FOOTBALL AMBASSADOR

By
EDDIE HAPGOOD

GCR BOOKS LIMITED
www.gcrbooks.co.uk

With thanks to
TONY, LYNNE & MICHAEL HAPGOOD
for their generosity and kind
cooperation in the
republication of their father's book.

First Published in Great Britain in 1945 by Sporting Handbooks Limited

This edition published in 2010 by GCR Books Limited
Registered in England & Wales – Reg. No.6949535
www.gcrbooks.co.uk

ISBN 978-0-9559211-2-4

Text and editing by Greg Adams and Colette Wittich

Printed and bound in the UK by
CPI Mackays, Chatham ME5 8TD

INTRODUCTION

A well-known photograph taken in 1937 shows our father, Eddie Hapgood, in a group of Arsenal players gathered around a television camera before the first televised game of professional football. Football footage, replayed countless times across our screens today, has changed modern expectations. In comparison, the black and white photographs of the great players of our father's era can seem static and the pre-war game a nostalgic memory.

Now we hope that this new edition of *Football Ambassador* will play its part in recreating the unique drama and achievement of the very different era when our father played. In the 1930s, the game had more physical contact than today, pitches lost their grass as the season progressed, and a player had to be strong just to head a waterlogged, laced-up leather football. There were no substitutes, so physical endurance and courage were at a premium. Yet, even in these difficult and demanding conditions, artistry of the highest level flourished. In these pages, the reader will also learn about the context for many footballing myths from the man who created them, whether leading the England team out in Rome in front of Mussolini, or resisting the order to give the Nazi salute in 1938 at the infamous Olympic Stadium in Berlin, where he led England to a 6-3 victory over Germany.

But *Football Ambassador* is much more than a historical document. Today, we can buy any number of football autobiographies. *Football Ambassador*, published in 1945, was the first. It is a remarkable account of the brilliant career of a slightly built Bristol boy who grew up to be the model footballer of his age and, in the judgement of many, the game's first modern footballer, a master of skill and tactics, a proven leader who was tough and brave. He tells his story with an energy and humour that reveals the qualities that made his fans and us, his family, love and admire him at home, in everyday life, and as the captain of Arsenal and England.

To our father, being a footballer meant being true to a whole code of honour - of loyalty and integrity, of striving for excellence, of overcoming physical challenges and pain by dedication and determination. His autobiography, *Football Ambassador*, tells some of the stories of a life lived by this code.

Tony, Lynne and Michael Hapgood

FOREWORD
By Sir Stanley F Rous
Secretary, The Football Association 1934-62
President, FIFA 1961-74

In this brief foreword it would be impossible to pay adequate tribute to the part which Eddie Hapgood has played in the development of Association Football during recent years, but after reading this autobiography, I feel sure that his many admirers will agree that his outstanding career fully entitles him to be styled a "Football Ambassador."

Readers of this book will visit many football grounds both in this country and abroad, will have the opportunity of seeing "behind the scenes" and will be introduced to numbers of sporting personalities. The accounts of these visits and meetings are Eddie's own and while I cannot pretend always to agree with his views, I feel sure that his experiences will be of interest to all footballers.

Hapgood has represented his country in more Internationals than any other Association football player and on his last appearance – the 43rd – at Wembley on January 27th, 1943 against Wales, H.M. King George VI congratulated him upon his distinction and subsequently graciously consented to autograph a photograph of the occasion.

When talking to those who join the ranks of professionals – an honourable calling – I always stress that they should strive to behave on and off the field as a model on which young players can mould their play and conduct. That, Eddie Hapgood has done. He joins those great players such as Harold Fleming, Arthur Grimsdell and Jesse Pennington, who contributed so much to the standard of British play.

S. F. Rous
1945

CONTENTS

LIST OF ILLUSTRATIONS

CHAPTER 1

HOW IT ALL STARTED

I was ten years old when I was presented at Court. Not my coming-out – but very nearly my "going-in." I was up before a magistrate on the terrible charge of playing football in the street. A hefty clearance (yes, even in those days I was a full-back) smashed a window, plus three milk bottles in formation on the sill. The lady of the house came out with the ball, and, after rating us, said we could have it back if the guilty offender owned up. I stepped forward – and then a policeman arrived.

The magistrate ordered me to pay 2s 6d damages (Mother, of course, obliged), and then delivered me a lecture, ending in the words, "You really must curb this passion for kicking a ball about, otherwise it might get you into trouble."

But I went on kicking footballs about, and the only trouble it has got me into is the thought of sitting down to write this book. However, I've always had the reputation of being able to stand up for myself verbally, so here goes to talk myself out of another spot of trouble.

After seventeen years in top-class football, I still don't feel any inclination to give up playing. The pair of football boots I have hung on to throughout the war – I shall throw them away some time, when they are no good, even for salvage – are still kicking a ball about. Seventeen years of the greatest game in the greatest company.

And I've had a grand time. Soccer has taken me to fourteen countries, and given me forty-three international caps for England, a record I treasure, two Cup winners' medals (another I lost on a disputed goal), five league championship honours, and made for me a host of friends I tried never to let down.

I say this with all sincerity. If I had my time all over again, I would still be a professional football – and, if possible, play for Arsenal.

Mighty Arsenal. The "Bank of England" team they've sometimes been called. The most publicised football team the world has ever known, and the greatest club side of all time. I hope I may be pardoned for dwelling awhile now, and later, on the Arsenal. I spent the greater part of my career as a member of the Highbury side. And, I think, in my small way, I helped to put them on the pedestal from which they will take a lot of knocking.

Everything happened to Arsenal. Rarely a day passed that we didn't read something about ourselves. Some of it was far-fetched, a lot of it ridiculous, but all of it was Arsenal. But all the time the papers were writing about our luxury stand, our cocktail bar, new club colours, special training methods, "cotton-wool diet for the players," our private train, and all the thousand and one everyday items which made sport headlines, Arsenal were delivering the goods.

In ten seasons (between 1930 and 1939) we carried off the League championship five times, won the cup twice, were runners-up, and were only three times out of the first three in Division 1. A great record.

But I'll tell you about that later. It's nice to look back, to let events of the past string themselves on to the necklace of the present. Many have been the questions since I gave up the game – what was my sharpest memory, who was the greatest player I ever met, what was it like at Highbury; and dozens of similar queries people on the outside looking in always ask the favoured few who mix in the top company.

In this book I'll try and answer those questions. And if you get as much pleasure reading about my experiences as I had while they were happening, well, we'll all have had a good time.

Apart from my street escapade, I played little football at school. To be exact, only two games. Toward the end of my stay at the council school, efforts were being made to introduce more P.T. into the school curriculum. Football was also to be incorporated, so the headmaster told me to get a team together, and he fixed us up with clobber. We only played two matches, before I moved on to a higher grade school!

So it wasn't until I had finished school some years and had gone out into the world to earn a living, which consisted of driving a milk cart for my brother-in-law, who had a dairy near Bristol, that I took the game seriously. Then I got the bug and whipped up my old horse every Saturday morning to get away for a game with a local club, St. Phillip's Adult School Juniors. Mostly I played full-back, but on one occasion went centre-forward in the second-half....and scored four goals in ten minutes!

It was while playing for St. Phillip's that I was spotted by a director of Bristol Rovers and given a trial at Eastville in a reserve match against Taunton United on May 7, 1927. I was then eighteen. I was chosen in my regular position, left-back. Opposing me was Treasure, the old Bristol City full-back, who had been my schoolboy hero and who had, not long ago, left Bristol City for Taunton. He played outside-right that afternoon, probably to test me. I must have impressed somebody. A few days later I was asked to sign professional forms.

And here, after all these years, is the true story of that offer. I have read many times that Bristol Rovers let me slip through their hands, but this is what really happened. A Rovers' director came out to the dairy with a professional offer of £8 0s 0d a week, and a place in the first team. I asked what I would do during the summer. "I have a coal business," replied the director, "and I can fix you up driving a coal cart." Gently, but firmly, I ushered him out of the house. I figured there was a social distinction between driving a milk cart and a coal cart.

A month or so later George Charlesworth, then a player at Kettering, turned up with an offer from the Town of £4 0s 0d a week winter wages, and £3 0s 0d in the summer. In addition, I was told I could continue working at the dairy during the close season. That sounded better, so I signed.

My first display for Kettering must have been appalling. In their report of the match the local paper suggested that the club had bought a "stumer." But things improved, and, after a dozen games, Bill Collier, the Kettering manager, called me into his office and introduced me to a chubby man in tweeds, whose spectacles failed to hide the shrewd, appraising look from his blue eyes. I didn't know it then, but I was to see this man many times before he died so tragically seven years later.

"Eddie, this is Mr. Herbert Chapman, the Arsenal manager," said Bill Collier. "And the other gentleman is Mr. George Allison." And so I met two of the men who were to play such a major part in my future football career.

Herbert Chapman didn't say anything for a few seconds, then shot out, "Well, young man, do you smoke or drink?" Rather startled, I said, "No, sir." "Good," he answered. "Would you like to sign for Arsenal?" Would I. I could hardly set pen to paper fast enough. I believe Mr. Chapman paid Kettering roughly £1,000 for my transfer - £750 down and a guarantee of about £200 for a friendly match later on. But I didn't worry about that at the time.

That remark of Mr. Chapman's about smoking and drinking impressed itself on my mind, for I have never done either during my career....with the exception of drinking occasional toasts at banquets and other functions. I have even drunk to our cup winning success in lemonade!

Incidentally, I played in the "Hapgood guarantee" match against Kettering and never kicked a ball right. Maybe I was too keen to show that "local boy" had already made good. The teams that day make interesting reading now:

KETTERING: Imrie; Allison; Jamieson; Duncan; Barrie; Collier; Charlesworth; Starsmore; Simpson; Dunsire and Cairns. (Imric, Barrie and Simpson later went to Crystal Palace, Starsmore to Coventry, while Collier was, of course, the club's player-manager).

ARSENAL: Moody; Mackie; Hapgood; Molloy; Cope; Haynes; Ashcroft; Buchan; Maycock; Diaper; Arnold.

The game was drawn 0-0, although Peter Simpson nearly got a winner in the last few seconds.

I played in another friendly against Kettering later on. Or rather, I should say, in half a friendly. I still have a cutting, taken from the local Kettering paper, which tells most of the story. I think it is worth repeating.

"The next time I go to see a match on the Rockingham Road ground at Kettering, I shall insist on being accompanied by Sherlock Holmes, the "Big Four" from Scotland Yard, and a leading member of the British Magical Society. Though I have no intention of causing any undue alarm in the camp of the faithful followers of the "Poppies" (nickname of the Kettering team), I feel it incumbent upon me to warn them, at the close of a thrilling season, that the green patch which covers the playing area conceals a treacherous quicksand, wherein players disappear and are never seen again.

Kettering were entertaining the Arsenal in a friendly fixture, and, with the exception of a goal or two that happened along in the first half, all went well (though I believe the diminutive Mitchell had some trouble with his shorts – they seemed to fit too tightly round his ankles). It was after the referee blew the whistle for the refreshment interval that the tragedy happened. Two strapping Arsenal players – David Jack and "Happy" Hapgood - vanished into thin air. Presumably , the quicksands had swallowed them up, not even

5

a tuft of hair could be traced, and the crowd stood aghast when the Arsenal re-started. No David Jack; no Happy-go-lucky Hapgood.

In their places appeared two substitutes, mysteriously recruited from some sort of Arsenal "pool" held in reserve (like a battalion in billets) somewhere behind the grandstand. People wondered; they whispered in queer undertones. What happened to Jack? Where was Hapgood?

If there had been another adjournment before the end of the match, I should not have been surprised to see the Arsenal team re-enter the arena with a brand new forward line, three halves borrowed from the Scottish League, two backs from West Bromwich, and a goalkeeper on loan from Newcastle United!

I was just beginning to wonder whether the police had authorised the issue of the usual £500 Reward notices, when a powerful voice nearby informed the world that Jack and his friend had merely dropped out to give two other Arsenal men a chance to kick the ball!"

Heavily sarcastic, but amusing. What had happened was that David and I needed a run-out, but were also due at Burnley in an important League match the following day. So Herbert told us to play the first half only at Kettering, and then catch a train for the North.

CHAPTER 2

FINDING THE "LADY"

And so, one Saturday morning in October, 1927 (the 27th, it was), I packed my grip and travelled up from Kettering to play my first game for Arsenal – against Chelsea reserves at Highbury. It seems a far cry back to those days when I was a slim lad with shock hair, tight trousers and pointed shoes. And very self-possessed, for was I not a man of the world? I was not even dreaming of the fame that awaited me in London – I knew it was there ready for the taking. But my confidence was to be badly shaken before the train reached St. Pancras.

The only other occupant of my carriage was a burly man with all the signs of a pugilistic career stamped on his face. We sat, as English travellers do, eyeing each other, but saying nothing. Then, a few seconds before the train started, a party of half-a-dozen men got into the carriage. Cheery fellows they were, and before very long we were all chatting away as if old friends. Among the late arrivals was a meek little man who soon produced a pack of cards, which, he said, he had picked up on his travels in Russia. He talked awhile about that country, then suggested a game of cards to while away the journey. Nothing loath, and bubbling over with good nature at being taken for a man of experience, I agreed to wager a small sum against my skill in picking the Queen of Hearts out of three cards the little man laid out on his lap. The big man with the battered face also had a flutter, and so it went on until the train reached St. Pancras. Then the *seven* got out together – and I realised that all my money, including the £10 0s 0d I had received from Arsenal as a signing-on fee, was gone. It is the only time I have tried to "Find the Lady."

I was really sunk now. My first time in London, I had no money and I was due to play my first match for Arsenal in

7

a couple of hours. While I was pondering on my misfortunes and bad luck in not picking the right card, I felt a tap on the shoulder and turned to meet a stocky little fellow with humorous eyes – not that I was in the mood for humour then – who, before I could speak, said, "Is your name Hapgood?" I nodded. "Right first time. My name's McEwan, "Punch" they call me at Highbury. Pleased to meet you." Was I pleased to see him? I could have cried on his shoulder. Then I blurted out my story tale and Punch laughed loud and long. But he said kindly, "It's all right, son. You are with Arsenal now and everything will be taken care of." Punch was a great scout and never told anybody about my initiation into "big time" gambling.

Well, that's how it all started. Years after, I asked Punch how he recognised me so quickly. "Easy," he said, "the Old Boss told me what you would look like!" It must have been the pointed shoes and tight trousers!

Punch was always a great pal of mine, the first of my many friends at Highbury, and I was terribly shocked to hear of his death in May, 1942. Punch was appointed coach to Arsenal (who had dropped the "Woolwich" from their name the previous year when they moved from Plumstead) in 1914, and, when I joined the staff in 1927, had become an institution. His greatest soccer memory, I believe, was playing in the most sensational Cup Final of all time. He was full-back for Bury when they beat Derby County 6-0 at the Crystal Palace in 1903.

Mr. Chapman was once heard to say that Punch's cheery face was worth almost a goal start to Arsenal when the lads were feeling a bit down at half-time. But there was a time when his cheerfulness failed to work the oracle. We were in the Wembley dressing-room, trying to fill in those hour-long last few minutes before the strains of "Abide With Me" warn you the ordeal of going out to the Cup Final pitch is near at hand. Along the corridor our opponents, Newcastle United, were probably feeling as bad as we were.

But old Punch tried his best to keep our spirits up, and played over and over again on the portable gramophone Herbert Chapman had given us, "Happy Days Are Here Again." Until, suddenly, the "recital" ceased, when a nerve-racked player burst out, "Turn that record off, or I'll kick it out of the room." Poor old Punch, he was only trying to help!

I make no apologies for dwelling at length on Punch. He helped a lot, particularly that first day when I arrived at Highbury. I thought of that day long before, as we walked into the dressing room after beating Sunderland on September 2, 1939. The balloon floating over Gillespie Road was casting its shadow on things to come and the feeling was that the war could not long be delayed. I must have subconsciously known that afternoon was a turning point in my life, but I didn't realise it was the last big game I should play at Highbury. The boys were quiet in the bath. Quietly we slipped away with no heart, even to talk of our big win. Even Ted Drake, who, after scoring four goals, was always good for a few wise-cracks, had little to say.

On the Monday morning, with the war twenty-four hours old, I walked into the ground. Workmen were already there, with pneumatic drills roaring, making air raid shelters. Highbury was putting on its war paint.

Tom Whittaker has, perhaps of all the people who helped me at Highbury, been my closest friend. It was he who, not long after I got into the first team at Highbury and my head was growing fatter than my body, accompanied me when I announced my intention of going upstairs to see Herbert Chapman. And it was Tom, with the Old Boss, who argued long and patiently with me when I said I was fed up with football and wanted to go back to my milk round at Bristol.

Tom and I often chat about those days. And, looking back, I can see how his calm judgement and guidance played

9

its part in many similar hectic moments. It was to Tom that I turned in the 1943-44 season, the season which was to give me the International record, but which was to cost me my place in big football. And that was because, for once, I wouldn't take Tom's advice.

It doesn't matter now to admit that, like that morning coming up from Kettering, I gambled the wrong way. Halfway through the season I badly tore the muscle of my left thigh, but went on playing. With no opportunities for treatment or regular training, the leg got steadily worse. At last, I managed to get away from my Service duties to see Tom, by now Flight-Lieut. (and later Squadron-Leader) Whittaker, who was holding an important post on the technical side of the R.A.F. He told me to take a rest from football for six weeks, but I argued I wanted to play, so, much against his will, he strapped up the leg again and sent me on my way. I went on playing, but lost form and my place in the England, Royal Air Force and Arsenal sides. Well, that's life. You make a decision for the best, and it turns out the worst thing you ever did. But it made me realise later how much I had owed to Tom Whittaker.

After the Old Boss died, Tom had a lot to do with keeping the Arsenal side on an even keel. The new manager, Mr. George Allison, had the hardest job in the world following a man like Chapman. But Tom knew the methods which had made us a great team, and to him it was we turned in the weeks which followed. Tom has always given the same service to Mr. Allison as he gave to the Old Boss, and, personally, I think it was more than the average luck of a club to have two men like Chapman and Whittaker in one life time.

Herbert Chapman was a great planner who loved to sit up to the early hours with Tom Whittaker and, perhaps, a newspaperman or two, arguing tactics, angles, theories; whose first thought was for the players – "if they are settled then I can be comfortable too" was his code; who never made a bad "buy"; who could not tolerate dirty play or slacking – the man who made Arsenal.

Herbert, in his early days a professional footballer, loved the game and understood it as well as anybody. He never forgot his first connection with the game, and, although his main interest was to give bigger and better football to the public, he always had a soft spot for the pro.

His death in 1934 left a gap which, to my mind, has never been adequately filled. I shall long remember that day. We were due to play Sheffield Wednesday at Highbury. I was shaving at my Finchley home when Alice Moss, wife of our goalkeeper, came rushing in in an awful state. While shopping she had seen the placards which shrieked to the world "Herbert Chapman Dead." I still had one side of my face lathered, and so stunned was I by the news that I stayed that way for quite fifteen minutes. Then I finished my shave and hurried along to the ground to find the news was only too true. Highbury backstage was like a morgue that afternoon and we weren't very keen on the job of playing football.

It was a long time before we recovered from that tragic day. Herbert Chapman, the man who had done so much, and who still had so much to do. We may never see his like again.

As I have already said, when Mr. Chapman went, Tom Whittaker tried to fill the gap for us. Tom is a great lad and a gentleman. He looked after us as if we were a flock of unruly sheep. Even Alex James was less boisterous when Tom was around.

Looking back, I realise I must have been a difficult customer for Tom. I rarely trained with the other lads, preferring to slog away by myself. It was not that I didn't get on with the rest of the players, or thought that I knew more than Tom could teach me, but I felt I knew just how far I could go when I was training myself. Often I trained in the empty stadium. If ever there's a ghost at Highbury he'll probably look like me.

Tom used to let me go my own sweet way. I'm glad he had that trust in me. I was always training. One of my favourite tricks was to take a ball over the railings on the terracing, bang it up the slope and intercept it as it came bobbing down, cannoning off railings and the wooden piles. Surprising how helpful this became – but be careful of your ankles if you try it.

Tom always says I'm the toughest player he ever met. When I first arrived at Highbury I weighed only nine stone, six pounds. I was probably the lightest full-back on the books of a league club at the time. Less than a month later I played my first senior game for Arsenal, against Birmingham at St. Andrews on November 19, 1927. We drew 1-1. The following week I was chosen for the big London "derby" with Spurs, but, to my intense disappointment, the match was "fogged" off. I was then left out of the side for a while, as Horace Cope, whose place I had been taking, was passed fit again.

About this time I was causing a lot of worry to the club by frequently being knocked unconscious while heading the ball, particularly on heavy grounds.

All sorts of reasons were put forward to answer this phenomenon – I even heard said that I had no bone on the top of my head – but Tom Whittaker found out what was wrong. "You're too light," he told me, "and we've got to build you up." At that time I was a vegetarian and old Tom decided I'd got to eat meat. My first meat dish was a plate of thinly cut ham. I got that down and progressed by various stages until I was eating steaks as thick as *Whitaker's Almanack* – and coming up for more. I still eat meat, when I can get it, but don't smoke or drink. Which once brought a wisecrack from a pressman that, although I never drink, I've been under more bars than he had!

Football is a tough game and hard knocks are to be expected. I've had my share with concussion three times, both ankles broken and my Roman nose broken three times. But the worst injury I ever suffered had nothing to do with football. It happened this way.

In his early days my son, Anthony, suffered from chronic catarrh, and, at night, in the bedroom there was always burning a bowl of oil throwing off a vapour which helped his breathing while he was asleep. One night he cried out suddenly and I leapt out of bed to help, only to make myself a nuisance all round, for I knocked the burning oil over my stomach and lower limbs, and I'll say it hurt. I was terribly burned and I think the doctor was doubtful whether I'd ever play football again.

But after a while lying in bed became a bit irksome, so I asked Tom if he would help me. He agreed and so I was taken to Highbury and lay on the rubbing slab in the dressing room, with Tom my only attendant, while the boys clattered in and out. He dressed the burns at hourly intervals and just let me lie there. He even washed and shaved me. I must have been a nuisance but he never said anything. He never would, anyway. After six weeks I was able to walk about again, and felt a lot better. So much so that I told Tom I was going to play again. At first he flatly refused, but, after a while, I talked him round. So Tom concocted a leather harness which I wore strapped round my body, and, muffled up with this and pounds of cotton wool, I was able to take my place in the Arsenal side. Only Tom could have done that for me.

Another time he saved me from losing a leg. Going up to play at Sunderland, I told Tom that my knee, which had been kicked the previous week, was giving me a bit of pain. When we got to the hotel at York, where we were breaking the journey for the night, he had a look at it, and, to our horror, found it had turned septic, and that there was a red line of blood poisoning visible above the knee and running up my thigh.

Tom is at his best on urgent jobs such as this, and, immediately, got to work with hot fomentations. Before proceeding, he made an ink mark on my thigh with his fountain pen, and said, "Eddie, if it gets above that line you will be in serious trouble." He worked until four o'clock in the morning, slapping on the boiling fomentations….and I played that same afternoon at Sunderland with my leg strapped up.

It is not generally known that Tom did as much to keep Fred Perry in big tennis as it was possible for any man to do. The English tennis champion came back from Australia, suffering from an injury nobody seemed able to diagnose. Tom heard about this, and asked Fred to come along to Highbury and let him have a look at things. A few days later Perry was out training on the pitch at Highbury with the Arsenal lads! I understand it was as much nerves as anything else where the highly-strung Perry was concerned. Tom, of course, trained our Davis Cup team from 1936 until the war put an end to big tennis.

And what of Mr. Allison? When he took over at Highbury as secretary-manager in May, 1934, he was already known to the public by reason of his broadcast commentaries. As I have already said, he was entirely different from the Old Boss. Originally a newspaperman, he had, and still has, a keen publicity sense. If he hasn't the football knowledge Chapman possessed, he is shrewd. Mark you, he was probably the luckiest football manager of all time. When Mr. Allison took over, Arsenal were running on top note, and he kept them there. Not as successful a buyer as the Old Boss, Allison, nevertheless, made his mark in football history by paying the biggest transfer fee (up to the moment) when he bought Bryn Jones from Wolves.

Mr. Allison is a rotund gentleman with a commanding presence and a deep "wireless" voice. Genial, an eloquent speaker with a nice sense of humour, he is universally popular in the football world. Newspaper boys, in particular, dote on him, for they are always sure of an interesting story for their columns after a few minutes in his company.

I had my ups and downs with Mr. Allison, the worst when I was nearing the end of my career with Arsenal during wartime. I was hurt that he so readily agreed when Luton asked permission to play me at the start of the 1943-44 season. I would have liked another term with the Reds. Quite a few people blamed Allison for the slump that season, but it would be as well to remember that the players were growing old together, and, great though we were as a peacetime combination, wartime football, with its attendant travelling difficulties, is another matter.

Many clubs had cause to bless the ultra-keen publicity sense Allison possesses, when they received fat cheques as their share of a record Cup or league gate.

Mr. Allison is the first to tell a story about himself, so perhaps, he won't mind my passing on these two. Shortly after he was appointed manager of the club, Mr. Allison came into the team discussion, and, naturally, took charge. He was very brief and summed up the following day's match, thus: "You are playing Sheffield Wednesday tomorrow and the danger man is Charlie Napier. You, Crayston (Jack Crayston, our international right-half) have the job of marking Napier – wait a moment, let me finish and then give me your views (this as Jack tried to break in) don't leave him, and don't let him have the ball. And now, Crayston, what have you to say?"

"Only this, Mr. Allison," mildly returned the player, "Napier plays for Sheffield Wednesday but we play Blackpool tomorrow!" Mr. Allison, with so many things to think about, had unconsciously mixed his matches.

And the other story, which, I think, is Mr. Allison's favourite, also concerns the Wednesday. He was in the directors' box on the Wednesday ground at Hillsborough, watching us play in a sixth round cup-tie, and with the score at 1-1 and a quarter of an hour to go, things were getting a bit anxious. He sat there watching every move, and, as the game swept from end to end, nervously chewed at his fingers.

Suddenly, a broad Yorkshire voice called out, politely, "Mr. Allison." Even in the strain of the moment George could not refrain from showing that dignity which is a part of him. "Yes, what is it?" he replied, turning to face the enquirer. "Stop bitin' tha' nails," was the crushing retort, which raised a gale of laughter, in which, I might add, George joined.

Joe Shaw, assistant to both Herbert Chapman and George Allison, is out of the same mould as Tom Whittaker. Kindly, helpful, always ready to lend an ear to a player's troubles, he played his part behind the scenes at Highbury for many years. Many's the piece of good advice I've received from Joe, particularly in the days when I was a hot-headed young player going places fast, and trying to get there a little too quickly. He is now at Chelsea.

One kindly action I shall always remember. After the Old Boss died – and his passing hit Joe hard, if not harder than it did us – he sent each of the players connected with the Chapman regime, a framed tribute, containing a photo and a grand verse. It occupies an honoured place in the drawing-room of my Kettering home. I have included a reproduction of it later in this book. It may interest you to know that the words of the tribute were written by Thomas Moult.

CHAPTER 3

WE HEIL HITLER

When war came to black out Europe, I realised, at long last, my touring days were over. Unless, of course, I was chosen as a member of another kind of side, to play a different game, the only game the Nazis know how to play. And as the war progressed, and the capitals of the world came into prominence, either as battle grounds for land armies or targets for the various Air Forces, I had a feeling of sorrow that those cities I had known and admired would never be the same again. The lovely places I had visited, and where I had experienced so much pleasure and been received so handsomely, were being blasted up by the very roots.

I've been to most of the countries which were finally caught up in the world conflict....I've played for England before 110,000 screaming, yelling, heiling Germans at the Berlin Olympic Stadium, the day we humbled the pride of Nazidom on the world's most luxurious ground. I've kicked a football into Mussolini's lap in Rome, and experienced the worst refereeing of my life at Milan; I've been to Switzerland, Rumania, Hungary, Czecho-Slovakia, Holland, Austria, Belgium, Finland, France, Norway, Denmark, Sweden and Yugoslavia. I've eaten garlic until I felt I never wanted to eat another thing in my life; I've seen the oil wells of Ploesti (before the U.S. Liberators got among them), the gondolas of Venice, beautiful Vienna, and all the great cities of Europe. I've been in a shipwreck, a train crash, and inches short of a plane accident....but the worst moment of my life, and one I would not willingly go through again, was giving the Nazi salute in Berlin.

And here's the story of that salute, which made headlines for every sporting sheet in the world. The story starts in 1936. That year England competed in the Berlin Olympic Games, held in the fabulous stadium, built for the sole purpose of impressing the world with Nazi might – hundreds of millions of marks were spent, not only in the building but in propaganda to put over the Games.

Mr. Stanley Rouse, the Football Association secretary, went over in charge of the English amateur side, which competed in the soccer tournament. Early on, the question of the salute to be given to Hitler at the march-past was causing some anxiety. After most of the other countries had decided on the Olympic salute (which is given with the right arm flung sideways, not forward and upward like the Nazi salute), it was arranged that the English athletes should only give the "eyes right". Mr. Rous told me afterwards that, to Hitler, and the crowd stepped up in masses round him, the turning of the head by the English team probably passed unnoticed after the outflung arms of the other athletes. So much so that the crowd booed our lads, among them Arsenal colleague, Bernard Joy, and everyone seemed highly offended.

When it was our turn to come into the limelight two years later over the same vexed question of the salute, Mr. Wreford Brown, the member in charge of the England team and Mr. Rous, sought guidance from Sir Nevile Henderson, the British Ambassador to Germany, when our party arrived in Berlin. Mr. Rous reminded Sir Nevile of his previous experience and suggested, as an act of courtesy, but what was more important, *in order to get the crowd in a good temper*, the team should give the salute of Germany before the start. Sir Nevile, vastly relieved at the readiness of the F.A. officials to help him in what must have been an extremely difficult situation, gladly agreed it was the wisest course.

Mr. Wreford Brown and Mr. Rous came back from the Embassy, called me in (I was captain) and explained what they thought the team should do. I replied, "We are of the British Empire and I do not see any reason why we should

18

give the Nazi salute; they should understand that we always stand to attention for every National Anthem. We have never done it before – we have always stood to attention, but we will do everything to beat them fairly and squarely." I then went out to see the rest of the players to tell them what was in the offing. There was much muttering in the ranks.

When we were all together a few hours before the game, Mr. Wreford Brown informed the lads what I had already passed on. He added that as there were undercurrents of which we knew nothing, and it was virtually out of his hands and a matter for the politicians rather than the sportsmen, it had been agreed that to give the salute was the wisest course. Privately he told us that he and Mr. Rous felt as sick as we did, but that, under the circumstances, it was the correct thing to do.

Well, that was that, and we were all pretty miserable about it. Personally, I felt a fool heiling Hitler, but Mr. Rous's diplomacy worked, for we went out determined to beat the Germans. And after our salute had been received with tremendous enthusiasm, we settled down to do just that. The only humorous thing about the whole affair was that while we gave the salute only one way, the German team gave it to the four corners of the ground.

The sequel came at the dinner table in the evening after the game, given by the Reich Association of Physical Exercises, when, with everybody in high good humour, Sir Nevile Henderson whispered to Mr. Rous, "You and the players proved yourselves to be good Ambassadors after all!" And that's what really happened.

Harking back a few weeks before the match, I can recall the excitement which seemed to suffuse the whole of the English soccer world. All who were likely to be connected with the forthcoming German trip, and many others beside, sensed that this was not merely a football match, but something deeper, a challenge from Germany which England

19

had to answer, and not only answer, but to defeat. I can't explain how I felt at the time, but although we are professional footballers, we also have human feelings like other people. We read the papers and listen to the wireless, and I fancy most of us had the same thoughts where Germany was concerned. That, to put it mildly, and in sporting language, they weren't playing the game. We remembered the happy, laughing fellows from Austria who had given us such grand games at Stamford Bridge and Vienna, and what had happened to their country, and to them, since. And so, although it was with mixed feelings we awaited the announcement of the names of the players who were to take part in this game, it was also, as I said, with mounting excitement.

At last the names of the party were released, and the Press Association flashed over the team: Woodley (Chelsea); Sproston (Leeds United); Hapgood (Arsenal); Willingham and Young (Huddersfield); Welsh (Charlton); Matthews (Stoke City); Robinson (Wednesday); Broome (Villa); Goulden (West Ham); Bastin (Arsenal); Cullis (Wolves); Bateman (Brentford); and Clifton (Chesterfield). A nice looking side and one we thought capable of beating any team we were matched against. But there was still a question mark about this match. A sort of feeling of taking on an unknown quantity.

I was glad I was in the team, and doubly so because, again, I was chosen to captain England, in what looked like being the toughest match of my career.

But for all the mixed feelings some of us may have had about the trip, it was a merry party which left Liverpool Street Station on the Wednesday night preceding the game, en route to Harwich, the Hook of Holland....and Berlin. There was Stan Cullis, discoursing deeply on various topics – I can't remember whether he had taken up Esperanto by then – Ken Willingham, the irrepressible humorist, Don Welsh with his bubbling laugh, and the rest of us.

A pleasant trip, with most surviving the sea crossing, and the first sight of a German in his own country for many of us when we crossed the frontier between Holland and Belgium, a green-uniformed Customs official.

Naturally, as soon as we were able, we all got down to a bit of sightseeing in Berlin, but I think the majority of the party were a little disappointed there was no fighting or lorry-loads of Stormwehr rushing hither and yon! However, we survived and, next morning, travelled down to the Olympic Stadium with Tom Whittaker for a leg-loosener. Coming from a country where the majority of clubs boasted large-sized stadiums, and also having played on the world's largest football ground, Hampden Park, we were, nevertheless, astonished by this wonderful enclosure. It was a grand sight, rather like a Hollywood film-set, as it lay, huge, magnificent almost, and yet rather garish, in the blazing sun. The turf was as good, perhaps better, than Wembley, but there was more space all round the pitch than at our Cup Final Stadium – which is claiming something.

The only moan we had was that the German authorities (could it have been arranged with malice aforethought, we wondered) had assigned us to dressing-rooms at the very top of the huge main stand. It took us about half-an-hour to climb to our quarters, and, from this viewpoint, the pitch looked like the dregs of crème-de-menthe in a giant bowl.

Next day, at an official "get-together", we had our first close-up view of the German eleven with whom we were to do battle. Some we already knew, but I sensed, even in this informal atmosphere, the lads were sizing up our opponents of the morrow. Stan Matthews confided afterwards that he thought Muenzenberg, my opposite number, and Stan's immediate worry, was looking older than when they last met, at Tottenham three years earlier.

This, then, was the mighty German team, which had been chosen with as much thoroughness as if it was destined to be Hitler's personal bodyguard. For months past, the Nazi soccer chiefs had been holding trials, had searched and tapped the football resources of the Reich, had discarded this player and that, and had even gone into over-run Austria for the pick of their talent, in an endeavour to discover a combination capable of taking on England's best.

Then the whole party, officials, players, photographers and the rest, had been spirited away to a secret hide-out in the Black Forest for a fortnight's special training, under ideal conditions, until the team thought and moved as one man.

I thought of these things as I eyed this bunch of arrogant, sun-bronzed giants, who looked, and felt, confident of doing what Hitler also thought possible when he marched against the world a year later….beating England.

Well, we knew what we were up against, and I might say we were a thoughtful bunch when we returned to our hotel that evening. But looking round my team, I also felt confident. I argued to myself that there were enough football brains in the side to beat eleven Germans, and, after all, we were playing for England, which also meant something. So with that I went to bed in a happier state of mind, and slept the sleep of the just, or at any rate, the near-just!

Berlin was *en fete* for the match, and on the Saturday, almost for the first time since our arrival, we seemed to come into things a little. Hitherto, not much notice had been taken of us, but there was a crowd to see us leave our hotel for the Stadium, and they even raised a cheer. We changed in our "skyscraper" quarters and led the way on to the field, rather in the manner of the challengers taking the water first in the Boat Race.

You could feel the jubilant, triumphant tone of the 110,000 crowd when the German team ran on to the field. A terrific roar greeted them, then a roaring crescendo of "Sieg Heil" and "Heil Hitler." The crooked cross of Nazidom floated everywhere, and the handful of Union Jacks fluttered bravely in that overwhelming, vulgar display of black and red.

Hitler wasn't present, but in the Fuehrer's box were Hess, his deputy, Ribbentrop, Goering, and Reich Sport Leader, von Tschammer und Osten, together with Sir Nevile Henderson.

Goering, who had just been appointed Field-Marshal, was resplendent in a cream uniform embellished with yards of gold braid. He wore as many medals as I had international Caps, and stuck on the ledge of the box in front of him were the largest pair of field glasses I have ever seen. He kept using these to watch the play, but didn't seem to know much about what was going on. I was told afterward he was staring at the English goal while we were scoring at the other end and Sir Nevile leaned forward to tell him he was looking the wrong way!

It was a scorching day, but the turf was in perfect condition and as I trotted up to the centre to meet an old opponent, Szepan, the German captain, for the spin-up, I said to myself, "Eddie, my lad, if you can't play football on this stuff, you'll never play anywhere."

Better pens than mine have described the game, but I knew we were going to win when, after fifteen minutes, Cliff Bastin, my only Arsenal colleague in the side, cracked home a beauty. Germany equalised shortly afterward, but we weren't worried and led 4-2 at half-time, young Jackie Robinson, who played a blinder, Broome of the Villa and Stanley Matthews having scored. Robinson got another after the interval and Len Goulden finished the match with a terrific left foot volley from way out – one of the hardest-hit goals I've ever seen, and one which made me leap into the air with delight. We had won 6-3, perhaps one of the greatest wins of all time by an English soccer side. Certainly the most satisfactory.

I was a proud and happy man that afternoon when we trooped up the stairs, four flights, to our dressing-room after the match. In the light of future events, I wonder what the grim-looking, and obviously very disappointed, Nazi party officials said to their players when it was all over. Probably took their names and sent them to Russia when Germany attacked the Soviet!

This is how we turned out that day, I shall remember that team and that match for a long, long while: Vic Woodley, Bert Sproston, myself, Ken Willingham, Alf Young, Don Welsh, Stan Matthews, Jackie Robinson, Frankie Broome, Len Goulden and Cliff Bastin. Interesting about the left wing pair. The only previous time they played together was in a schoolboy international game.

I often wondered during the war what happened to the German team we played that day. The only reference to any of the players I spotted in the autumn of 1943, when a small paragraph, which Reuters picked up from the German News Agency, said that Albin Kitzinger, who played left-half, and who was also in the Rest of Europe side at Highbury, was injured in a heavy daylight raid on Schweinfurt by Flying Fortresses.

CHAPTER 4

MUSSOLINI – "BULL'S-EYE"

But to other things, and the ball that nearly laid out Mussolini. I was playing my first game for England, in Rome, on a sweltering May day in 1933. I knew nothing about the incident until a friend told me after the match, or, maybe, I would have been worried. Apparently, in clearing a particularly heavy attack, I fired the ball into the crowd. Musso, sitting in profile with his chin at the angle favoured by all dictators since Nero, failed to see the ball coming and it crashed against his tightly fitting uniform, just above his lunch. My friend, who had quite a lot of difficulty in keeping his face straight, told me Musso, when he got his breath back, looked as if he wanted to kill the man who had outraged his dignity. But somebody must have told him to behave himself, for I never heard anything officially. But I often wish it had been something more lethal than a football that I kicked into his lap that afternoon.

Incidentally, I had the experience of getting even closer to Mussolini on that trip. During one of our sightseeing tours, the whole party was taken to his palatial home on the Palazzia Venezia, and, after a look around, were told we were going to be photographed with the great man. We massed in the great banqueting hall, and, at last, Mussolini swept in, chin held up at what must have been an uncomfortable angle. He was simply dressed in a black coat and pin-striped trousers, and I was rather gratified to find that I was a couple of inches taller than him! Still in this same grim, fierce mood, he posed with us, and, later, autographed our photos.

Something always seemed to happen on those Italian tours. Perhaps they were the most wearing, and you had, particularly, to be on your best behaviour, but we got a lot of fun out of them.

This Rome match had another humorous memory for the English lads who took part. It was a tremendous struggle with the crowd at white heat excitement all through. The match was played at a terrific pace in the blazing sun. The speedy Italian forwards were giving us all they knew, and, at last they took the lead through Daussi, their left-winger. Then bedlam really broke loose. Frantic Italians stormed over the barriers, and made a bee line for the beaming capering scorer, who was being mobbed by the other home players.

They grabbed Daussi, hugged and kissed him, and when one of the enthusiasts produced a bunch of flowers, garlanded him with them and escorted this living, floral tribute back to the centre line, while the rest of the crowd behind the barriers bayed their appreciation. Out of the corner of my eye I saw Harry Hibbs, who was keeping goal for England that day, turning back from his task of plucking the ball out of the net to stare with amazement at this crazy, comic scene. Daussi was one of the importations from South America, and, if he never did anything else, he earned his money that day.

But my greatest memory of Rome was meeting His Holiness, Pope Pius XI. The F.A. party were taken to the Vatican on a tour, and, while we were studying the famous place we had heard so much about, one of the Italian officials informed us that the Pope was holding an audience of pilgrims, and that we were going to be privileged spectators. There was a buzz of excitement among the party as we moved into the huge hall where pilgrims from all parts of Italy, and, in fact, from all over the world, were gathered together awaiting what must have been the greatest moment of their lives.

And then, preceded by minor officials of the Catholic Church, the Pope appeared. The pilgrims sank to their knees and he moved among them, murmuring a blessing, as, one by one, they kissed his ring. He looked a great man, and there was a kindly expression on his lined face.

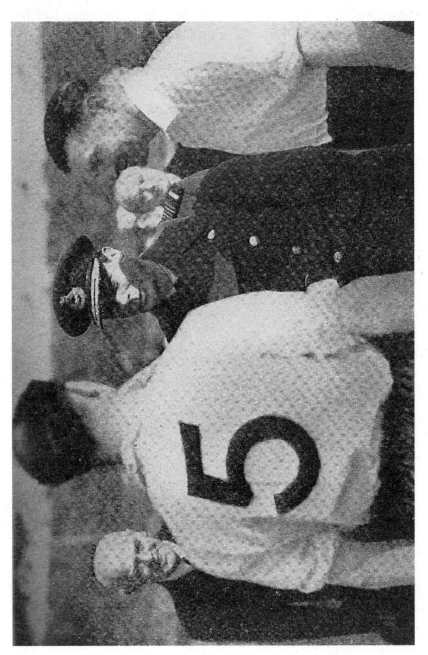

I meet the King

Captain of Arsenal. Following the author on to the field at Highbury is Roberts.

The Old Boss

The infamous salute at the Berlin Olympic Stadium. The England team are in the white shirts.

A legacy of the *"Battle of Highbury."* Tom Whittaker at work on the England captain's broken nose after the match with Italy, 1944.

Il Duce poses. Mussolini later signed this photograph, taken during the 1933 F.A. tour, for the author. Fifth from the right is Herbert Chapman, and standing on Mussolini's right is Sir Frederick Wall.

The author following Roy Goodall on to the field at Rome for his first international game, England v Italy, 1933.

The England party outside the Dolder Grand Hotel, Zurich, after beating Germany.

CHAPTER 5

BATTLE OF HIGHBURY

An injury to Tom Cooper, the second captain I played under in the England eleven (Roy Goodall was the first), gave me the opportunity of leading England for the first time, against Italy at Highbury on November 14, 1934. During the previous summer Tom had led the side on my second overseas tour, to Hungary and Czecho-Slovakia, where we lost both games. After the Budapest game against Hungary, when we only got one goal against their two, I heard Tom Cooper say to referee Wally Lewington, "They went through us like chaff".... and that was after we had played ourselves to a standstill! Frank Moss later complained in the dressing-room, "I thought they weren't allowed to charge. I've spent 90 per cent of the match rolling in the dust!"

When the England team for the Italy match (billed in Italy as the "most important football match that has been played anywhere in the world since the Great War") was chosen, surprise was occasioned by the inclusion of five Arsenal players; Moss, Copping, Bowden, Bastin and myself. A few days before the match, Tom Cooper dropped out through injury, and George Male was brought in, to make the Highbury contingent six! Meanwhile, several of the newspapers began speculating as to who would captain the side in Cooper's absence, and I was gratified to see my name appear among the "possibles."

But there was still to be another "shock" for the soccer fans before the team took the field. On the Monday Fred Tilson, the chosen centre-forward, was forced to drop out, and after George Hunt had been invited and had to refuse owing to injury, Ted Drake was notified he would be required....making a grand (from our point of view) total of seven Arsenal players, an all-time record for an England international team!

Then, a few hours before kick-off time, I was told I was going to captain the side, for the first time, which made me very happy that this great honour should be granted on my home ground. The selected team was: Moss, Male Hapgood, Britton (Everton), Barker (Derby County), Copping, Matthews (Stoke City), Bowden, Drake, Bastin, and Brook (Manchester City). The other Arsenal "representatives" were Tom Whittaker, in charge of the team, and George Allison, who was giving a running commentary from the stand.

I got a great thrill leading the side on to the familiar field, and, after the National Anthems had been played, introduced two distinguished visitors, the late H.R.H. Prince Arthur of Connaught and Signor Grandi, the Italian Ambassador, to the England team. Then I trotted up to the middle for the spin-up with Monti, the Italian captain, in what turned out to be the dirtiest football match I have ever played in.

Away we went, and, in fifteen minutes, had the match (apparently) well won. Inside thirty seconds we should have been one up, but Eric Brook's penalty effort was magnificently saved by Ceresoli, the Italian goalkeeper, and a very good one, too. But Eric made up for that. After nine minutes, he headed a cross from Matthews into the net, and, two minutes later, smashed in a second goal from a terrific free kick, taken just outside the penalty area.

Our lads were playing glorious football and the Italians, by this time, were beginning to lose their tempers. Barely had the cheers died down from the 50,000 crowd, that I ran into trouble. The ball went into touch on my side of the field, and, to save time, the Italian right-winger threw the ball in. It went high over me, and, as I doubled back to collar it, the right-half, without making any effort whatsoever to get the ball, jumped up in front of me and carefully smashed his elbow into my face.

I recovered in the dressing-room, with the faint roar of the crowd greeting our third goal (Drake), ringing in my ears, and old Tom working on my gory face. I asked him if my nose was broken, and he, busily putting felt supports on either side, and strapping plaster on, said it was. As soon as he had finished his ministrations, I jumped up and ran out on to the field again.

There was a battle going on, each side being a man short – Monti had also left the field after stubbing his toe and breaking a small bone in his foot. The Italians had gone berserk, and were kicking everybody and everything in sight. My injury had, apparently, started the fracas, and, although our lads were trying to keep their tempers, it's a bit hard to play like a gentleman when somebody closely resembling an enthusiastic member of the Mafia is wiping his studs down your legs, or kicking you up in the air from behind.

Wilf Copping enjoyed himself that afternoon. For the first time in their lives the Italians were given a sample of real honest shoulder charging, and Wilf's famous double-footed tackle was causing them furiously to think.

The Italians had the better of the second half, and, but for Herculean efforts by our defence, might have drawn, or even won, the match. Meazza scored two fine goals in two minutes midway through the half, and only Moss's catlike agility kept him from securing his hat-trick and the equaliser. And we held out, with the Italians getting wilder and dirtier every minute and the crowd getting more incensed. One of the newspaper men was so disgusted with the display that he signed his story "By Our War Correspondent."

The England dressing-room after the match looked like a casualty clearing station. Eric Brook (who had his elbow strapped up on the field) and I were packed off to the Royal Northern Hospital for treatment, while Drake, who had been severely buffeted, and once struck in the face, Bastin and Bowden were patients in Tom Whittaker's surgery. Cliff by the way, Barker, Copping and Ted (in his first international) played like heroes.

That night, at the banquet, the England team looked a sorry sight. With my nose still plastered and a nasty feeling in my mouth over the whole affair, as well as a splitting headache, I was called up to receive the tokens from Signor Grandi. As I wended my way through the crowd, I passed the table at which sat my assailant of the afternoon. He looked me straight in the eyes....and laughed. I'm glad I am a pretty even-tempered fellow, or I would have gone across the table at him. But he wasn't worth it. I thought then that I never wanted to see an Italian again in my life, but of course, I played at Milan five years later, when there was another fist-casualty, George Male.

Some months after the Highbury match, it was made known that the probable reason for the display of the Italians was that they were under a terrific inducement from Mussolini. Each man had been promised that if they won, he would get a substantial money award of something like £150, an Alfa-Romeo car, and what was more important to them, exemption from their annual military service. They didn't deserve any of it, and, although they scored twice in the second half, they didn't get enough goals to beat us.

Well, that was the dirtiest game I ever played in. I never played dirty football myself, first because I never wanted to, and, second, that type of game never gets you anything but injuries and suspensions.

Another game best forgotten was against Hull City in the semi-final the year Arsenal went on to beat Huddersfield in the Final. After drawing 2-2 at Leeds, we met Hull the following Wednesday at Villa Park. David Jack got a goal in twelve minutes, and, from then on, the game went from bad to worse. Some of the Hull players tried to play without the ball, and we were all profoundly relieved when the final whistle went, and we were booked for Wembley.

We, at Arsenal, always knew we were due for a tough (never dirty, mind you) game when our league fixtures took us against Villa or Huddersfield. I think of all the teams we met annually, they were the hardest to beat. There were times, of course, when we won easily, notably the match at Villa Park when Ted Drake set up a First Division goal-scoring record by netting each of the seven goals by which we beat Villa. Incidentally, in this match Ted only had nine shots at goal, and one of these was brilliantly saved at point-blank range by Morton!

It was at Villa Park that I got my nose broken for the first time. This game, the injury apart, was one of the most exciting I ever played in. They got a goal early on, we equalised, they went ahead, we squared it, Villa made it 3-2, and again we drew level. All in the space of the first half-hour. Then Billy Walker broke away, and Joe Hulme chased him back. A faulty tackle, Billy went over, and the referee gave him a free-kick. Walker took the kick and crossed the ball high in front of our goal. I went up for it, and, in trying to clear at the same time, Herbie Roberts' elbow crashed into my face. I came to, holding the upright, then I fainted again, and found myself in the dressing-room, with Tom, inevitably, working on me.

"Is my nose broken?" I demanded of Tom.. Trying to cheer me up, he replied, "I don't think so." So I said, "If it's broken, I'm not playing this game any more." Tom said quietly, "You had better have a look in the glass." I staggered across to the mirror, and there saw that my nose was spread sideways across my face. Strangely enough, I didn't feel so bad then, and said, "Well, if that's a broken nose I can carry on." Tom put the pads and strapping on, and I ran out to continue this terrific match, with my shirt (we always changed colours against Villa) looking rather sanguinary.

40

Villa, by this time, were leading 5-3 with about twenty minutes to go. With a full side again, Arsenal plugged away and David Jack got one of his inimitable goals....4-5. Then he missed another chance almost on time, and we had lost. But those were the sort of games we didn't mind losing.

We always said we could never beat Sheffield United on their ground. And they often beat us at Highbury, too. We finally laid the bogey when we had to win at Bramall Lane to secure the League championship. We did this by 3-1, and I don't think we were really troubled by the Sheffield United menace any more.

One Sheffield match provided me with a secret which I have kept to myself until this day. It was my second game for Arsenal, and Harry Johnson and I went for the ball together, with me facing my own goal. I tried an overhead kick to clear, but he ran into me at the same moment and the ball shot off my foot like a rocket, straight into the Arsenal net. Johnson's name went into the goal-scoring list, and, I have never actually been quite sure whether his foot hit the ball as well, I didn't take the credit away from him!

West Bromwich sometimes had a knack of cramping our style. They are one of the few clubs who persistently depute their wing-halves, instead of the full-backs, to mark opposing wingers. We always had to work out a special plan when they tried this stunt against us.

Mention of the Albion, reminds me of the time we made a hurried dash to get away from the Hawthorns in order to catch a fast train to Town. Time was so short at the end of the game that we didn't even stop for a bath or change, but dashed to the charabanc, which was waiting with steam up, to take us to the station. A little later you might have seen eleven Arsenal players wandering up and down the train corridors in playing kit, and carrying towels, looking for wash-basins in order to scrub off the mud we had carried away from West Bromwich!

A similar instance occurred after a match with Everton. Again, we raced straight from ground to station, and, clad in long white bath-towels over our kit, stood shivering on the station, waiting for a train that was fifteen minutes late!

CHAPTER 6

MY LAST TOUR

The last tour abroad I made, as a player, was in the May of 1939, only a few months before the war. I was again selected to captain the side to visit Italy, Yugoslavia and Rumania. Perhaps as it was my last, and is still fresh in my mind, you will bear with me if I enlarge on it a little.

Although we didn't know it at the time, that particular tour was, perhaps, of even more political importance than the German trip the year before. I have since learned that not very long before the England party was due to leave for Italy, it was odds on the Foreign Office preventing us fulfilling the fixture, in view of the prevailing uncertainty on the Continent.

With the Italians on a hair-trigger, and chanting about 8,000,000 bayonets, and backing Hitler up to the hilt, it would have been extremely unfortunate if, through us, or, rather, through our presence, there had been another of those international "incidents" by then becoming all too common.

However, after long discussions with Football Association officials at Lancaster Gate and Whitehall, all details were settled and permission was granted for us to carry out the proposed programme.

After a long and hard season, we weren't concerned with the political aspect of the tour, but were looking forward to a restful holiday in sunny Italy, with, of course, a little football thrown in. There was quite a bunch of us at Victoria Station to catch the 2 p.m. Dover Express on Tuesday, May 9 – sixteen players, Tom Whittaker, of course, Messrs. B. A. Glanvill, T. Thorne, H. Greenwood and S. F. Rous of the Football Association, a number of club directors and press representatives.

As I said, our main interest was the scenery, with the prospect of football in the background, but, looking back on it, and knowing what I do now, I can quite well imagine the gathering anxiety of the F.A. officials as every revolution of the mighty wheels of the Orient Express took us nearer and nearer Italy, and beyond, the Balkans.

But all was well. From the frontier, all the way to Milan, the Italians said it with flowers. When we ran into Stresa to stop for customs inspections the carriages suddenly became flower-filled bowers. Beautiful Italian girls threw baskets of all kinds of blooms at us, and even hung garlands round our necks. Gradually, the atmosphere worked up to something approaching semi-hysteria, as this thistledown people endeavoured to show us how welcome we were. Among the floral gifts were sprays of carnations each containing a card bearing the words, "Stresa welcomes you." Which brought the crack from one of the players, he shall remain unknown, "They might have said 'for Stresa jolly good fellow!!'"

And so it went on. At wayside stops the process was repeated, until we began to feel like the centre-piece of a gangster funeral, or, better still, like film-stars. If we had been welcomed at Stresa, Milan overwhelmed us. Thousands of excited youths and girls mobbed us for autographs, and it was some time before we could get away to our hotel, where things became just as hectic.

The crowd, by this time, was reinforced by some of Musso's cheer-leaders, who led the chant for the English team to show themselves. Nobody felt like facing the wolves, so we signed ourselves in and went upstairs to our rooms. George Male and I were room-mates on this tour, and we had a palatial suite between us, also a balcony.

The combination of the roar outside and the balcony suggested something to me, and I said to George, "I'll give them something to Viva about." With that classic remark, I

44

threw open the window, stepped out on to the balcony and gave the crowd a quick flip of my arm, the nearest I could get to a Fascist salute. In a moment I wished that I had stayed inside. The roar almost knocked me back into the room and was redoubled as I vanished. I suppose they liked my balcony-scene impersonation of Mussolini, for no stones or other lethal weapons were tossed through the window!

We had a little sightseeing in the two days remaining before the match, including a trip out to Lake Como, where we saw the football stadium built out into the lake. These really were lovely trips, and I thoroughly enjoyed seeing sights I probably never would have, had I not been able to kick a football about. (I wonder if my old friend, the Bristol magistrate, will read this!)

There was the usual visit to the Cenotaph, where I , as captain, placed a wreath on the Unknown Warrior's tomb, and inevitably a tour of inspection to the local Fascist headquarters.

Our hopes of a sunny holiday were not being realised, as on the Friday morning, heavy, cold rain set in. But although it affected our sight-seeing, it boded well for the match on the morrow, as none of us fancied playing on a concrete surface.

We had a pleasant surprise next morning when a solid phalanx of English supporters arrived at the hotel and clamoured to see us. They were from Malta, and had made the trip just as Arsenal supporters would go by excursion to Sheffield or some such place. And we were almost as delighted to see them as they were of the opportunity of seeing English League stars in person. Many of the party were Maltese, and, looking back, I'm glad we were able to give them a little enjoyment, with the Italians playing hosts, in view of what happened when, later, the Italians tried to smash their gallant little island.

It was still pouring when we got to the new stadium, which was filled to capacity with a 70,000 crowd. But we were used to rain on a Saturday afternoon and it didn't bother us. What was new, however, was that instead of the lone policeman "guarding" the corners of the ground in England, whose main function seems to be to give the crowd a laugh when they kick the ball, there was a close-packed line of carabinieri spread round just back of the touchline, inside the high wire netting erected to prevent bottles and other gifts being thrown to the players.

The carabinieri had fixed bayonets on their carbines, and each wore a spiked Uhlan helmet, which had been bought from the Germans at the end of the Great War!

Dr. Bauwens, the German, was in charge of the match and one of his decisions, when Italy took the lead against the run of play in the second half, must remain, for all time, the classic of incompetence. I remember that moment as if it happened yesterday, and I don't suppose many people who saw it will forget it, either.

Andreolo, the Italian centre-half, banged a ball down the middle toward Piola, the centre-forward, and George Male, who were standing with their backs to our goal. They went for it together, and it was odds-on George, for he was slightly the nearer the ball. As they went up together, Piola slipped, and, quick as a flash, back-handed the ball over his shoulder into the net. That was bad enough, but it was altogether an unlucky moment for my Arsenal colleague, for, in following through, Piola caught Male a beauty just over the eye. Of course, we protested strongly about the whole affair and Bauwens even went over to consult his linesman. But, he too, must have been blind, for the goal was allowed to stand. Unbeknown to us on the field, up in the Royal Box Mr. Rous was having the hardest job of his life politely refusing the Italian Crown Prince's request that he should accompany him (the Crown Prince) to the field to tell Dr. Bauwens that the goal was illegal! Next day we saw a picture on the front page of the leading Milan paper, showing the Crown Prince explaining to Mr. Rous exactly how the goal was scored by Piola's fist.

All ended satisfactorily for us. In the last five minutes Stan Matthews got away on one of his wriggling runs, and Willie Hall equalised after a defender had blocked Len Goulden's shot.

Another memory of Dr. Bauwens in that match was the huge coin he produced for the spin-up. A whole host of officials, led by Signor Grandi, and photographers, accompanied Meazza, the Italian captain and inside-left, and myself to the centre-spot. There was a heavy wind blowing the rain straight down the field and I was hoping to win the toss so that the lads could play down with it in the first half. Bauwens showed me the huge coin, and I indicated the side I wanted to call. The referee spun-up, and, as the coin landed, Grandi pointed the way he wanted the Italians to kick. I stopped that by showing Bauwens the coin had come up the right way for me. So, after all that fiddling, I got my way and we started with the rain and wind at our backs.

But all the disappointments of the afternoon were forgotten later on when we attended a fine banquet at which bonhomie and good wishes were the order of the evening. George Male came in for quite a lot of leg-pulling, for his eye, by this time, looked like something in technicolour gone wrong. But a placid sort of chap is George, and he took it all with a smile, albeit rather one-sided.

The British Ambassador attended the banquet and an Italian General was in the chair. In his speech, he dwelt at length of the friendliness of the Italian people for England....less than a year later they marched against a stricken France, and a backs-to-the-wall England. However, this book deals with soccer, not socking, so we'll say no more.

Next day we left for Venice, and so on to Yugo-Slavia.

CHAPTER 7

GARLANDS AND GARLIC

Although we arrived in Belgrade at the crack of dawn, there were hundreds of football enthusiasts to welcome us. And, also, the smell of garlic – strongly overcoming the scent from the myriad flowers which filled the station. It flowed out in waves, and engulfed us as soon as we stepped out on to the platform into the crowd. Early morning is not the time for over-effusiveness, but the Slavs were so happy in their welcome, almost childlike, that we could do nothing else but fall into their mood. Anyway, it was a happy augury for our stay in that land of turmoil.

There were speeches, the majority of which we didn't understand, while the crowd milled around. The morning newspapers carried messages of welcome. I append one, thanks to Mr. A. C. Davis, the West Ham director, who accompanied us on the tour, and later presented each of us with an interesting little booklet-diary of our trip. Interpreted, this is what it said:

WELCOME

"Illustrovani Sport cordially welcomes the England football team to Belgrade. How cordially it is difficult to put into words.

For years we have waited for the moment when the chosen representatives of the 'Home of Football' would measure themselves at their full strength against our eleven, which, at least in enthusiasm for the game, yields nothing to them.

As true sportsmen, we think less of the result of the game itself, but it is natural on this occasion, when we are faced with the most dangerous opponents the world provides, we should be anxious to give of our best, and prove the strength of our young Yugoslav football. We know that our guests and opponents, also as true sportsmen, ask neither more or less.

We wish them a pleasant stay in Belgrade and a hard match, which will provide fine football for tens of thousands who have come to see the greatest match of their lives."

Well, that was a fine start, anyway, but the main job, at the moment, was to get to the hotel for a wash and breakfast. Most of the lads succeeded in fighting their way to the motor-coach, but I was separated from the party and, eventually, walked to the hotel. I didn't need to ask the way, for the crowd literally carried me along with them.

I needed that hotel badly. A hot bath was the only thing that would get rid of the smell of garlic. And here I nearly had a 'fight' with a newspaperman. The room I was booked into had a bath, the only suite on the floor, and the pressman, in as bad a state as I over the garlic, was casting covetous eyes at it. But I was adamant, pausing only to promise him second use of the bath!

We had nearly two clear days before our match, and, naturally, got down to sight-seeing at once. On the Wednesday we were escorted to Oplenae, about twenty-five miles from Belgrade, to the church erected in memory of King Alexander, who was assassinated in Marseilles. It was a beautiful building, and, for some reason, I couldn't help thinking of the newspaper pictures I had seen some years before of the boy King Peter, leaving a quiet little school in England to return to his native land to rule in place of a father he had lost by a violent death.

Poignant relics of that tragedy were to be seen in the church. The patriots had taken the King's clothes, with the ghastly bullet holes and bloodstains, and laid them reverently in his shrine.

On from Oplenae in a conducted tour of the grape district and a trip over a wine factory or distillery, or whatever it is called. This was interesting, especially as we all received a bottle of wine as a souvenir! It was with pleasant thoughts in our minds we bade farewell and moved on to Arandelovac, where we saw another kind of 'liquid'….the mineral spring baths. Nobody seemed very anxious to take away a bottle of that!

Yet another banquet that night, at which Mr. Glanvill gave a further instance of his after-dinner speaking capacities. I also made a speech, of a different sort….a broadcast. An outside broadcaster came up to my table, carrying a trailing mike, and asked if I would say a few words on the forthcoming match to the Yugo-Slav people. I am afraid it all sounded rather superior when I said:

"Good evening. I hope you will turn up to see us play. We have brought a very strong team, and I am sure you will enjoy the football." They did….because they beat us 2-1!

I almost forgot. During the afternoon, we had another interesting experience, with an unfortunate sequel for myself and two other members of the party. Here, let me say I am a great tea drinker, and, like many an Englishman on the Continent, have cried in vain for a cup 'made just like I like it at home.' Only once during my wanderings abroad did I get anywhere near a decent cup….and that was in Belgrade.

As often was the custom on these trips, we were invited to the house of the British Minister, Sir Ronald Campbell, for an afternoon reception. We sat around in the beautiful fully furnished drawing-room after being received by the Minister and his wife, and tea and cakes were served. I remarked, rather audibly, after my first cup, that it was the best I had tasted since leaving home. Lady Campbell happened to overhear the comment, and, as we were leaving, said to me, "I'm glad you enjoyed the tea. Here's a little present for you." It was a whole pound packet of Lyon's tea! Talk about corn in

Egypt. So I told two other great tea-drinkers, Tom Whittaker and Ken Willingham, and off to the hotel we dashed as fast as the cab would take us.

As soon as we were settled, we called the head-waiter, and, handing him the precious packet, asked him to make us a 'proper pot of tea'....and not just to dip the leaves in and out of the pot, as we suspected had been done during our stay. So he hurried away and we sat and waited. At last, he returned, bearing on a tray a small white teapot, which he handled as if it were the Yugo-Slav Crown Jewels. I, as host, was deputised to pour out, and Tom and Ken sat licking their lips.

I'll draw a veil over the rest. The tea came out like syrup. The head-waiter had put the whole pound in that little pot!

And so to the match. We fielded the same team as against the Italians, although at one time it looked as if changes would be made, as quite a few of us left Milan carrying scars of battle. Chief anxiety to Tom Whittaker was Stan Matthews, who had jarred his hip-bone through an all-in tackle from Rava, the Italian left-back. But, after a try-out a few hours before the match, Stan declared himself fit, and we played as selected.

Things went wrong from the start. Stan told me afterwards that his leg went again in the first five minutes. In trying to do his shuffle-dart past Dubac, the Yugo-Slav left-back, he felt something give, and, for the rest of the match, was little more than a passenger. Stan wasn't the only one. I ran into trouble early on, tearing a ligament in my ankle, so that we virtually had only nine men.

That was bad enough, but although I rarely complain about the fortunes of a match, I must say we didn't have an even break from the referee, the Frenchman, Capdeville, who, not long before, had taken charge of the World Cup Final. Be that as it may, however, we lost the match.

When the Slavs scored after fifteen minutes, it was as if the whole of Belgrade had gone crazy. The noise lasted for minutes after the ball had been centred, and had a great tonic effect on the Slavs, who got stuck in with a vengeance. But we kept them out until the interval, and, four minutes after the break, we were level.

Frankie Broome and Tom Lawton did a perfect switch in the middle of the field, and Broome hit the ball home from a centre-forward position. We badly needed an impartial referee, but the breaks went to the other side, and they got the winning goal. A long pass eluded Cullis, and the left-winger, Perlic, ran on to belt the ball past helpless Woodley. That was that.

We played well, but not well enough. However, the enthusiasm shown by the Slavs at their victory was such that we almost (I said 'almost') felt glad they had won!

CHAPTER 8

AMBASSADORS

When we left Belgrade next evening on a fourteen-hour boat trip down the Danube, most of the lads were feeling a little jaded, and I, for one, knew that my football was over for the trip. Tom had given me a going-over, but I wasn't feeling so good.

Most of the party got up at 4am the next morning to see the famous gorge on the Danube, the Iron Gates. It was a lovely site, but we were all disappointed the Blue Danube was a sort of poetic licence allowed opera writers and composers of waltzes. It was brown. But the scenery on either side of the river was wonderful and kept the trip from being boring.

When we got to Turnu-Severin, the whole of Rumania seemed to be out in force to greet us, and all carried flags or flowers. Many of the flags were Union Jacks, probably home-made. In addition, there were two bands on the riverside, one a brave band of boy scouts, and the other, an ornate military affair. Both played God Save the King, one slightly faster than the other. And when the race had come to a galloping halt, they started all over again. We left them trying to blow each other into the river.

And so it went on. We were feted across Rumania. Everything was just as we had pictured it. There was even a gay gipsy orchestra to enchant us over lunch.

More flowers at Crajova, and, at last, we got to the capital, Bucharest. Thousands packed the station, the National Anthem was played three of four times, and, after more speeches of welcome, we literally fought our way to the coach waiting to take us to the hotel.

This hotel, I forget the name, but it was in the New part of Bucharest, was one of the loveliest I have ever been in. I had a whole suite, which was a mass of flowers when I arrived, and made me feel like a visiting monarch. And there was even a chambermaid to press my trousers every day!

Incidentally, here let me introduce an entirely personal note. I got the title for this book from the following welcome which appeared, in English, on the front page of one of Bucharest's leading papers. Here´s what it said:

"The Rumanian Football Federation has the honour of receiving, as guests, the British National Team, in view of a match which will be written with capital letters in the history of Rumanian football and be the most prominent sport event of the year.

Ambassadors from the land of the birth of football game, they arrive today in our capital town, bringing a token of the true friendship between the countries with common ideal, crystallised through historical bounds.

We all consider their visit as an opportunity to show to our players, as well as our spectators, the concretion of a sportive ideal, which we try hard to reach.

The moment when the British National Team reaches the Rumanian ground, together with the enthusiastic greetings of thousands of sportsmen and supporters, may we call them hearty 'Welcome.'"

Ambassadors they called us, and I suppose we were, in a way.

It was obvious that from the number of players nursing battle-scars, there would be changes for this, the final match. But that didn't stop us enjoying the sightseeing. The Continental people certainly laid themselves out to entertain us when we were on tour, and Bucharest was no exception.

On the Monday after our arrival in the capital, we all assembled early for a trip out to the oilfields. Our first port of call was an oilfield belonging to the Royal Dutch Shell Co. in the Prahavo Valley....and, strangely enough, it looked just like the oilfields we had only previously seen in a news reel!

It certainly was a great sight. Mile upon mile of giant derricks and wells, and were the Rumanians proud of them! As I have said in another part of the book, I bet it was even greater sight when the liberators got cracking on them during the war!

But our greatest thrill was still to come. After lunch we were taken to Pelash Castle, summer residence of King Carol and Mme. Lupescu. It was a fairy palace, a background such as you would expect in a Ruritanian musical comedy. Fantastic was the word for the whole lay-out. But ineffably lovely, and something to store in our memory chests.

We had a lot of fun next day. After the "official" business was over, we all went to a circus. And you can imagine us behaving like schoolboys on a treat, which we did. The occasion gave full scope to the humorists, Ken Willingham, young Leslie Smith and dry-as-dust Joe Mercer.

Shopping occupied our time on the morning of the match and one of the highlights was the dare offered to a player to go into a ladies underwear shop and ask to see a set of "unmentionables". It recalled the hilarious time we had in Budapest, when Ken Willingham accepted a similar dare. He marched into a beautifully furnished ladies shop, which had some extremely decorative assistants, and demanded to see the best of the stock, while we peered through the plate glass windows, watching the fun. Ken examined very nearly every dainty article in the shop before expressing dissatisfaction, and then stalked out to receive unstinted plaudits from the rest of us.

There were four changes for the match, Willingham, Matthews, Willie Hall and myself standing down for Morris (Wolves), Copping and a new left wing, Don Welsh, and Leslie Smith (Brentford), the latter making his first appearance for England. We "back-room boys" sat in the stand and took it easy while the lads out on the pitch fought all they knew to pull off our only victory of the tour.

The England side played brilliant football, with Stan Cullis and Len Goulden outstanding. It was Goulden who scored the first goal after five minutes, and then I knew we were going to win. Incidentally, this goal raises a point. I've never been over-fond of players being numbered, and here was a case for my argument that numbers do not materially help. Len scored from the outside-right position and, next day, the Bucharest papers gave Broome as the scorer.

The footwork of our lads was bewildering, and, disappointed though they were at the inability of their team to score, the Rumanian crowd paid full tribute. Frankie Broome was hurt in the second half, but stayed on and made the pass for the goal by which Don Welsh clinched the match.

And so my last tour ended, with me sitting in the stand. But it had all been great fun. All the same, we were glad to get home. War clouds were fast gathering over Europe, and, only a few short months later, some of our football friends became our war enemies, and later still our allies!

CHAPTER 9

MY GREATEST MATCH

My greatest match? Without hesitation I plump for the last England-Scotland international at Hampden Park before the war, April 15, 1939. Not for twelve years had England won at Hampden, and I figured our lads had a sort of inferiority complex when they went to Glasgow. Mind you, the whole atmosphere is enough to upset even the most iron-nerved. Glasgow is football mad at big match time. The Scots eat, drink, talk and dream football, and, naturally, the visiting side are affected by this atmosphere. The English teams which had been beaten were, on paper, good enough to hold their own, but there you are, not since gallant Jack Hill and his lads snatched an odd goal win in 1927, had proud Scotland been humbled on their own soil. This, then, was the setting for the match, and I was determined that, as captain, if it was humanly possible, we were going to come home with the spoils this time.

Going up in the train I used all my eloquence on the rest of the team and told them the Scots weren't supermen, that eleven Englishmen were as good as eleven Scots any day, and other things to the same effect. In the hotel I continued my pep talk, and carried on in the dressing-room until I must have hypnotised the team into thinking the match was as good as won.

We had a good team that day. Woodley was in goal, Morris of the Wolves and myself, backs, Willingham, Stan Cullis and Mercer, half-backs, Matthews, Willie Hall, young Tom Lawton, as big as a house and full of confidence, Len Goulden and Pat Beasley, my former Arsenal colleague, who so narrowly missed a cup winner's medal in 1936 and who, not long before this game, had been transferred to Huddersfield, were the forwards.

The Scottish team looked a good 'un; Dawson (Rangers), Carabine (Third Lanark); Cummings (Villa); Shankley (Preston); Baxter (Middlesbrough); McNab (West Bromwich); McSpadyen (Partick Thistle); Walker (Hearts); Dougal (Preston); Venters (Rangers) and Jackie Milne (Middlesbrough), another former colleague at Highbury.

We followed Scotland on to the field, getting the back-wash of the tremendous welcome which had lifted itself to the skies. There is no other soccer roar on earth like that of Hampden. It smashes back and forth across the world's largest stadium, stuns you, and leaves you gasping for breath. It's a great place to play in, but, much as they might appreciate English football, it's the blue shirts that get the crowd really crazy.

We won that day, we won as I knew we could, the better side, and with no hard luck stories. The match had its ups and downs early on, and Scotland got the first goal when Dougal, the quicksilver Preston forward, set the Scots aroaring. But young Pat Beasley, bless his heart, banged in the equaliser for us twenty minutes from time, when the Scottish defence was definitely struggling.

And that's how the score stood until a few minutes from time, when, although we were giving all we had, I began to despair of breaking that Hampden hoodoo. The crowd was still there. The great struggle had gripped them as it had got us, and pressmen, high up in that draughty eagles' eyrie in the Main Stand, have told me since that they found it difficult to concentrate their thoughts for the morrow's story in the electrical atmosphere. Every move was cheered. The Hampden roar smashed and echoed every time the Scots looked like attacking. The minutes ticked away, until there were only three left.

Then Len Goulden sent a long pass looping up the right touchline. Stan Matthews was there to pick up that ball. A bewildering juggle beat McNab, and he was away. The other England forwards ran into position while the Scots defenders dropped back to cover this new danger. Still Matthews went on. Cummings was in attendance now, but Stanley took the ball right down to the corner flag. Cummings tackled desperately, but Matthews, evading the outflung boot, cracked the ball into the middle. Big Tom Lawton was there, and his head flashed the ball into the top corner of the net, past the diving Dawson. We'd beaten Scotland.

It was a tragic disappointment for those fanatics over the border, but they took it like sportsmen and gave us a terrific reception as we trooped off the field, most of the players tired, nay, exhausted. It had been a hard game, but I was so elated that I ran round the field, patting my team on the back. Joe Mercer, who had played himself to a standstill, said he envied me my fitness. But we were, oh, so happy. And the scene in the English-room was like Mafeking night. Eleven grown men, most of them tried and tested in the international field, some with half-a-dozen or more caps to their credit, chattered and laughed like excited schoolboys. And I was the happiest of them all. I think that was the greatest playing memory, and I was proud to be an Englishman that day.

It was against the Scots that I gave away my only penalty in forty-three international games. It was also the first penalty awarded at Wembley. I don't make excuses, but it was a pure accident. However, it cost us the international championship that year, and made Scotland the first holders of the new King George V Silver Jubilee trophy.

For this match we go back three years from that great Hampden victory. We were leading Scotland 1-0 ten minutes from the end, and, I think, carrying all the marks of worthy winners, when young John Crum, playing in his first international, chased after a ball near the edge of the penalty area. I made him to be offside, and appealed to the referee, but kept moving all the same. I saw that Crum was trying to gather an awkward ball with his left foot. He shot a split second before my out-thrust foot touched his ankle. The ball went outside and Crum went down. Technically, it was a penalty, but I still think I was unlucky! However, it was an offence within the meaning, and I felt pretty miserable. It's not very nice giving away a penalty at any time, but at Wembley it seems a crime. Tommy Walker made no mistake….and I felt even worse. But the England lads took it very well and I got a little consolation when I read the papers the next day and found that nobody condemned me in print. But I did object to the abusive letters I received for some days after, all of them anonymous, and most of them containing phrases like "Dirty Hapgood" or "It serves Arsenal right." Incidentally, Jimmy Jewell, who awarded the famous "Mutch" penalty two years later, was on the line that day.

That was an unhappy Wembley, but I've had my share of triumphs on that great ground. I can't recall offhand the number of times I played there, but I figured in four Finals (one a wartime match against Preston, when we drew 1-1 and lost the replay 2-1 at Blackburn), twice on the winning side. Perhaps the 1936 Final, against Sheffield United (only ten days after the penalty incident) stands out most in my memory. And not because of the game.

On the Thursday before the game I was at Brighton with the rest of the team when I had a telegram from Bristol, saying, "Come at once, Mother dangerously ill." As soon as I told Mr. Allison about it, he packed me off home. It wasn't a pleasant journey, but I made it in record time. My Mother was very ill when I got home, and I stayed overnight. Next morning she seemed a little better and insisted that I go back and join the team, saying it was my duty and she would only worry if I didn't. I took a lot persuading, but eventually went, reaching Brighton early Friday evening. What wonderful people mothers are. Mine in particular. I am glad to say she recovered and is still alive and kicking.

But her illness weighed heavily on me all the morning before the match. I tried to shake off the depression I felt, saying to myself I can't do any good by letting the team down. But we played badly that day, and only the fact that fate was good to us gave us the cup. The match will go down in history as Ted Drake's final. Badly injured in the Welsh match at Wolverhampton three months before (when, incidentally, Arsenal had six men chosen), Ted was gambled on at Wembley. And the gamble came off. Wearing the world's biggest bandage on his left knee, Ted got the only goal of the match sixteen minutes from time. He told us in the dressing-room that when he received Cliff Bastin's pass, he knew it was now or never. And that when he hit the ball he knew it was a goal. But we had some scares before, and after, that goal. In the first minute Alec Wilson, our goalkeeper, usually the most unperturbed of fellows, dropped the ball at the feet of Barclay, the Sheffield United inside-forward. Barclay tried to push the ball sideways past Wilson, but Alec scrambled back to make a marvellous save.

With no score at half-time, we put into operation a plan we always saved for a rainy day. It was simple, but had to be carried out with split-second quickness. Ted Drake kicked off after half-time, a short pass to James. Bowden dropped back from inside-right and Jack Crayston, our right-half, who had been standing just outside the centre-circle, went racing through the United defence. Alex held the ball for a few strides, then banged it through perfectly to the swiftly moving Crayston. Jack coasted over the penalty line and let fly. It looked a goal all the way, and would have been one of the finest ever scored at Wembley. But Smith, the Sheffield keeper, made the save of his life, and we had to wait another 28 minutes before we knew the cup was ours.

We had tried that plan before several times, and, on the last occasion, against Wolves at Molineux, Crayston got even nearer to scoring. He hit the bottom of the post.

Other clubs copied that plan, with varied success. One of the best efforts I remember reading about was the smash-hit goal scored by Villa against Charlton in December, 1938, at Villa Park. On that occasion Iverson, the Villa left-half, went through from the centre and banged in a great goal. Eye-witnesses timed that effort as nine-and-three-fifths seconds from centre to back of net.

Incidentally, in the third round, the year we beat Sheffield United, we were drawn to play Bristol Rovers at Bristol, the first time I had played in my home town since the trial for Rovers against Taunton nine years before!

That match was very nearly the toughest of the whole cup series. We were one down in that roaring, excited atmosphere, and something just wasn't clicking in the Arsenal side. At half-time Tom gave us a good talking-to, switched Bobby Davidson to outside-left, brought Cliff Bastin into inside-right, and told us to go out and play like an Arsenal team. We did and got five goals in a row to win.

CHAPTER 10

"OVER-THE-LINE" GOAL

The luck doesn't always run smoothly, even for Arsenal, much as many people would have us believe, and it went against us in my second Final, against Newcastle United, in 1932. I still think their first goal should have been disallowed, but there's nothing I can do about it now. You remember the famous 'over-the-line' incident? Here's how I do.

Boyd, the Newcastle right-winger, cut inside to chase a long ball from Sammy Weaver, but I was there first and hit it upfield in the direction of Jack Lambert, our centre-forward. Meanwhile, Richardson had run out to the wing, when Boyd cut inside. Davison chased after the ball.

It was a long ball and I could see that it would be a desperately close thing if he were to catch it. Richardson, travelling at top speed, drew up to it and centred first time. But, by that time, we were appealing for an 'over-the-line' ball. At the same time, Allen cracked the centre into the net. But although we protested strongly to the referee (Mr. W. P. Harper of Stourbridge), he allowed the goal to stand. Allen got another later on, and we only scored one, through Bob John. But that's the luck of the game. It either goes one way or the other, and it certainly didn't go our way that year, for we had to turn out a reshuffled side in the Final, owing to Alex James breaking down at the last minute.

But my greatest Cup Final thrill was my first in 1930. I had only been in the Arsenal first team little over a year. We beat mighty Huddersfield that day, a great win, and a great moment for the Old Boss, who had made Huddersfield into a wonderful side, and who had then come on to make us an even greater team. That was the start of our great run. In the

63

next eight years we won the League five times, were runners-up once and finished third on another occasion. We also won the Cup and were beaten in the Final.

There was a lot of newspaper criticism about our first goal. One school of thought had it that Alex James committed an infringement when scoring. Others argued that it was quite legal. We of the Arsenal contended then, and I do so now, that it was fair. And a conversation I had with Tom Crew, who refereed the game, some time later, bears out that contention.

Alex was fouled somewhere near the penalty area, and, almost before the ball had stopped rolling, had taken the free-kick. He sent a short pass to Cliff Bastin, moved into position to take a perfect return, and banged the ball into the Huddersfield net for the all-important first goal. Tom Crew told me that James made a silent appeal for permission to take the kick, and he waved him on. It was one of the smartest moves ever made in a big match and it gave us the Cup. I contend that it was fair tactics; for if Alex had waited a few seconds for the whistle, the Huddersfield defence would have been in position, and the advantage of the free-kick would have been lost. Jack Lambert got the second goal late in the second half, also from a move by Alex.

During the second half there occurred one of those incidents which make a match of this kind even more dramatic. There is always a lot of noise in a Cup Final, but, above the hubbub, we heard a deep resonant booming, and over our heads, there floated into view the German airship, 'Graf Zeppelin,' looking like a great lazy trout as it drifted in the sunshine.

It flew the length of the Stadium, and dipped in salute to King George V. The players took one quick look, and then went on playing. To my knowledge, there was no stoppage and the ball didn't go out of play. For my part, my main feeling was of annoyance that anything could interfere with the game, and I wished it would go away! But it must have been a wonderful sight for the crowd.

On the Monday following the game we underwent almost as great an ordeal as playing at Wembley. The Mayor of Islington (Alderman W. E. Manchester) had invited us to a civic reception at the Town Hall, and we were going back afterwards to Highbury to play a rearranged League match with Sunderland.

We set off from the ground, with the Cup prominently displayed, several of us sitting on the top of the coach with our feet dangling through the open roof. Running through Islington, we came smack into a wave of soccer enthusiasm, the like of which I hadn't before seen outside a ground. Twenty thousand people lined the streets of Islington, and, from our coach, we could see women and girls being knocked down in the mad scramble for vantage points. Traffic was held up and police reinforcements sent for. Several people were injured, I believe, and one woman was taken to the Royal Free Hospital for treatment.

At the Town Hall, we were received by the Mayor and his Council. Standing on the steps while the crowd swamped us, I could see nothing but red and white— ribbons, flags and red berets. The noise was deafening from rattles, hooters, megaphones, bells and the cheers.

In the quietness of the Mayor's Parlour we recovered our breath, and then the Mayor expressed his pride, and, as he put it, the pride of all North London, that we had brought the Cup back to London after nine years (Spurs had won it last in 1921). Then the Cup was filled with champagne and the whole assembly had a sip to our success.

With time getting short before our match, we left by the side exit to escape the crowd. When we took the field, the Cup and the London Combination trophy were set out on show, and the Sunderland players lined up and cheered us, a handsome gesture. Then they proceeded to beat us 1-0, not at all a nice thing to do!

Tom Parker was our captain in the Huddersfield Final, and the honour of receiving the Cup from The King made up for his disappointment of three years earlier, when Arsenal lost to Cardiff City.

Parker was a grand full-back, and helped me a lot in my early days. But he also did something infinitely more precious than that. He saved the life of my son, Anthony. I have already said that Tony suffered quite a bit when he was very small, but one day, he had a really bad turn, and I could see he had to be got to hospital right away. My wife and I were in an awful state, but we got Tony dressed and I figured the best thing to do was to get him to the Great Ormond Street Hospital, where he had been receiving treatment for his ailment. I carried Tony and we hurried out to look for a cab. But there wasn't one to be found anywhere. Just as we both were getting frantic, the driver of a passing car hailed us. It was Tom Parker. When we told him of the trouble, he said, "Hop in. I'll get you there." And he was as good as his word. He drove us at top speed to Great Ormond Street… and the doctor told us later that another five minutes' delay would have cost us our son.

Although, I was in two cup-winning sides, I never had the honour of receiving the Cup from the hands of a member of the Royal Family. I nearly did so in 1936, when we beat Sheffield United, but actually "lost" the captaincy of the side on the morning of the match.

Alex James was elected captain of the Arsenal team at the beginning of the season, but, injured early on, he only played in one cup-tie in that series, being out of the side until passed fit a few hours before the Final. In his absence I took charge of the team. I have previously told of my dash to mother's bedside two days before the game and I suppose, in the excitement and flurry, Mr. Allison did not have a chance of suggesting that as 'wee' Alex was fit again, he should revert to the captaincy. So it was that I actually learnt of the change when I saw in a paper on the Saturday morning in the line-up of the Arsenal team— " James (Captain)."

That Wembley penalty. Crum (dark shirt nearest camera) goes down as Walker and the author (white shirt) watch Sagar, the England goalkeeper, dive for the ball.

"Over-the-line" goal. Allen heads Newcastle's first goal against Arsenal, Wembley, 1932, from the disputed centre by Richardson, extreme left. Arsenal players are, left, the author, Moss, Roberts and Male.

The intruder which interrupted the Arsenal v Huddersfield Cup Final, Wembley, 1930. An air photograph of the Graf Zeppelin flying over the Stadium during the match.

Arsenal v Sheffield United, Wembley, 1936. Ted Drake (on the ground, fourth from right) scores the goal which won the Cup.

En route for Wolverhampton for England v Wales, 1936. Left to right, Mr. S. F. Rous, Secretary of the Football Association, Male, Crayston, Drake and the author. In the doorway, Bastin and Bowden.

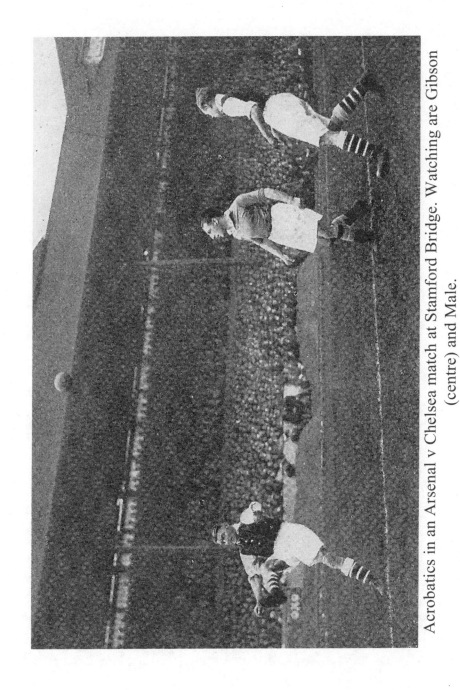

Acrobatics in an Arsenal v Chelsea match at Stamford Bridge. Watching are Gibson (centre) and Male.

The author's favourite picture. Young Tony Hapgood shows his skill at Highbury, watched by his proud father, Frank Moss and Alex James.

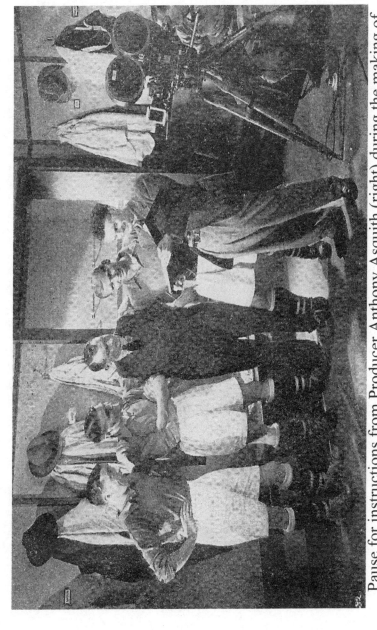

Pause for instructions from Producer Anthony Asquith (right) during the making of Gainsborough film "the Unlucky Number" at Twickenham. Clifford Mollison (left), the author, Tom Whittaker and Cliff Bastin go over their parts.

CHAPTER 11

I MEET THE KING

On the day that I set up the record for English international caps and was presented to His Majesty King George VI at Wembley, I must have been the happiest man alive. I had just been commissioned in the R.A.F., I remember. We lined up, as usual, in front of the Royal Box, with the Welsh team facing us. The King inspected the Welshmen first, then walked over to where I was standing at the head of the line of English players.

Usually, when distinguished persons inspect us, they just shake hands and pass on. But this afternoon, when Mr. Brook Hirst, Chairman of the Football Association, presented me to His Majesty, the King paused and said, "How many times have you played for England?" I replied, "Forty-three, Sir." The King then asked, "How old are you?" "Thirty-four, Sir" The King gave me a friendly smile, "The same figures reversed," he said. Odd that, until that moment I hadn't noticed the coincidence. Incidentally, it was also the thirty-fourth occasion on which I had captained England, another record.

It makes a great deal of difference when one of the Royal Family is up there in the box. Everyone seems to try and play a little better. And there's often much less stoppage for infringements.

That particular afternoon I took a little while to get into my stride. It's not often one has the privilege of holding conversation with the King before 75,000 people.

Incidentally, His Majesty did me the great honour of signing the photograph taken that afternoon of him speaking to me, and for that I am indebted to Lord Wigram and Mr. Stanley Rous for the work they put in for that great souvenir, which is my most treasured memento from all my years in football.

Another outstanding Wembley memory was the big 'Aid to Russia' game between England and Scotland on January 17th, 1942. When we took the field, heavy snow, which had fallen all the week, had been cleared from the sidelines, but the pitch still looked like a carpet of cotton wool. First thing that struck our eyes were the blue touchlines, standing out, broad and clear, against the white mantle of snow covering the velvety turf.

We lined up in front of the Royal Box for the usual pre-match inspection. Rumour had it that Mrs. Churchill was to attend but, under the wartime censorship ban, nothing had been published. Then Mrs. Churchill did appear, and we all felt the novelty of the situation of being inspected by a woman, a rare occurrence at a big soccer match. But the big thrill was to come. After she had walked along the lined-up England and Scottish players, she turned to face the arena as if to wait for the National Anthem. But there was a microphone in front of her, and she stared to make a speech, thanking everybody for their attendance making possible a large sum to go into the coffers of the fund.

It was obvious that Mrs. Churchill was very excited about something, and, suddenly, with the spontaneous, dramatic touch so often introduced into her great husband's speeches, she burst out, "But there's something else I feel you would like to know. My husband, Mr. Churchill, landed at Plymouth this morning after a 3,000 mile flying-boat trip from the Bermudas, and I am going along to Paddington later in the afternoon to welcome him back." Her last words were lost in a roar of cheering which continued until the strains of the National Anthem brought a hush. Mr. Churchill had arrived back safely, after the signing of the Atlantic Charter, and that was the crowd's way of letting him know, through Mrs. Churchill, how they felt about his great trip.

Naturally, in that excitement-laden atmosphere, something had to happen, and it did, for Jimmy Hagan cracked the ball into the Scottish net, within fifty seconds of the start.

That game also had another memory for me. I was hurt in a collision a few minutes before the interval, and had to be assisted to the dressing-room, which, at Wembley, always seems to be about four miles away when you are not feeling so good. I managed to resume in the second half, and we won comfortably by 3-0.

CHAPTER 12

I LOSE A "CAP" — AND MEDALS

Through one thing and another, I haven't many of my souvenirs left. I lost all my thirty gold medals while I was helping to make the film of "The Arsenal Stadium Mystery," at Denham. Burglars entered my house when nobody was at home and took the whole lot, leaving only my caps and a few shirts.

Some of my shirts I had previously given away. England shirts (with the badge taken off) are pretty useful for cricket. But one of them found a good home. Before the Wales-England match at Cardiff in 1936, I agreed to change jerseys with Willie Evans, the Wales and Tottenham left-winger, in the dressing-room after it was all over. But Willie was badly hurt during the game, and was rushed to Cardiff Royal Infirmary. I went round to the hospital before catching the train back to London, but Willie was too ill to see me. So I left my England shirt and came away.

I was, naturally, very sorry to lose all my medals, but, so too, was Tony. He used to find them great playthings, and many's the time my wife or I have rescued one of them from the garden, where my youngster had left it.

I am a great one for home life. I always liked to get back with the family after an away trip. Then I had to go all over the match again for Margaret, who is a great football fan. Of course, she has been to many games. I liked having her watch me. It makes quite a difference when your wife is interested in your work. I actually taught her to play football. We used to go out in the garden of our North London home, and I would put her through her paces. We enjoyed those games, and there was no magistrate to fine me half-a-crown if a window was broken!

79

My wife is a grand person, and, like all proud fathers, I think my kiddies are the best in the world. We have three, Edris Anthony, the eldest, Margaret Ann and Elizabeth Lynette. Margaret and I felt the separation keenly when I joined the Air Force. And when I started to play football soon after I was in uniform, I didn't get away much to see her. Actually, with one thing and another, we met for a total of only fourteen days during the first two years I was in the Air Force. One time, after a big representative match, I travelled back by a late train to Northampton in order to snatch a few hours with her, and found the last connection to Kettering (where she was evacuated) had gone. So I walked the fourteen miles home, carrying a football bag, and with a bad limp, a legacy of the afternoon's match. Who says it's all fun being a professional footballer in the Services?

Actually, the arrival of my son, Tony, lost me what would have been my first England cap, and, with it, an attractive Continental tour. I was invited to tour Austria and Germany with the F.A. party in 1930, when drawn matches were played in Berlin and Vienna, but turned it down when Mrs. Hapgood told me our first-born was on the way.

Three years later I got another chance to play for England, also on a Continental tour. This time I accepted, and played against Italy and Switzerland. But although I turned down one trip to Vienna, I did get there before the Nazis— in 1936, when we lost 2-1.

I would say that this was my unhappiest trip overseas. Not because I didn't enjoy the experience of visiting Austria, but because, being a football fanatic, I was so keen to make every match a winner. It was also my first meeting with another fanatic, the man who put Austria on the soccer map... Hugo Meisl.

Herr Meisl was so ultra-keen that he carried his schemes to great length, and stopped at nothing where his beloved team was concerned. The morning of our match, he called at our hotel and offered to show us the sights of Vienna. We jumped at the chance, and set off on what became the longest tour I have ever made of any city—on foot. We walked for miles, and I was beginning to bend at the knees when he said he must show us the birthplace of Johann Strauss. It was only round the corner, said the wily Hugo. But that corner stretched another two miles. And there we struck. Otherwise, we might still be wandering around Vienna. I thought afterwards that it might have been a ruse to tire us, but dismissed the thought as unworthy!

However, the Austrians started off the match at a terrific pace and over-ran us in the first fifteen minutes, during which they scored twice. Then we got a goal, recovered our touch and looked like not only saving the match, but winning it. But in the last fifteen minutes, Meisl (called by many 'The Chapman of the Continent') lay on the netting behind the Austrian goal and implored his goal-keeper and backs to take their time and kick the ball out of play. "We must win," was his oft-repeated plea.

In that last fifteen minutes the Austrian wing-halves were giving away a series of free kicks so that the whole defence had a breathing-space in which to get re-organised. I shall never forget the delirious delight with which that volatile little genius greeted the final whistle.

Another side to his character was shown after that game. Harold Hobbis, the Charlton winger, had been kicked in the stomach— quite accidentally— during the match, and was in some pain at the banquet that evening. Hugo Meisl learned of his trouble and spontaneously invited Harold to spend the next fortnight as his guest in the Austrian Tyrol. But we still had another match to play that tour, so Harold travelled on with us.

There was much murmuring in the British Press after that trip—we also lost on the Diables Rouge ground in Brussels—because, as they put it, there had been too many

Arsenal men included. Six of us—Bastin, Bowden, Copping, Crayston, Male and I—played against Austria, and the grouse was that we had had a very hard season (we won the cup, if you remember, and finished high up in the league).

Rudy Hiden, the great Austrian goalkeeper who nearly became a colleague at Highbury, had left his native country before that tour, but I played against him in Arsenal *v* Racing Club de Paris matches. Perhaps, of all the Continental goalkeepers, he was the best, and least showy. Most of them were like music-hall turns, and, of course, with charging not allowed in matches over there, they had plenty of time in which to posture and pose.

The refusal of the Ministry of Labour to allow Hiden to come over and sign for Arsenal in 1930 was a blow to Herbert Chapman, who had set his heart on having him at Highbury. The transfer fee between Arsenal and Hiden's club was arranged at £ 2,600, and the Austrian was to be guaranteed a job as a chef, and was also to receive the same wages as the other first-team players... £ 8 os. od. a week, and bonus money for a win or draw. Hiden was as keen as Chapman, and, taking up his headquarters at Ostend, made three trips to Dover, being stopped each time by the Customs authorities. The Ministry of Labour refused Hiden permission to stay here on the grounds that, if he were signed, it would mean the displacement and unemployment of an English professional. Perhaps it was just as well. There's plenty enough good players in this country to go round without importing them from abroad, so perhaps it was as well Chapman lost his game of Hiden-seek!

The Continental countries always made a fuss of their goalkeepers, perhaps, because, as I have just said, they got more chances to show off. Perhaps Zamora, the leaping wonder from Madrid, was the most boosted. I didn't play in the game with Spain at Highbury in 1931 when Zamora came over, but watched him pick the ball out of the net seven times.

Harry Hibbs, often my England colleague in later games, and who kept goal for England that day, once said that he was disappointed with Zamora, as he had expected to learn something from the 'greatest goalkeeper in the world,' as he was called. Harry told me that on his form that day the Spaniard wouldn't have got into any First Division side.

To my mind, Harry Hibbs was the best goalkeeper I ever saw, although Frank Moss ran him close. It was a treat to play with Hibbs behind you, and you always knew where you were. I have heard it said that old Sam Hardy, rated as the best-ever goalkeeper, used to tell his defence to keep out of the penalty area and give him some room. But there was nothing like that about Harry. He used to make a little mark in the middle of the goal on the six yard line, which served as a guide to his distance from the goal when he was taking a high ball or a corner. He was a first-class goalkeeper and a great fellow.

It was a great pity that injury forced Frank Moss to give up the game. He was, I think, the best goalkeeper we had during my association with Highbury….and Herbert Chapman used to say I was pretty good as well! The Old Boss insisted that I was a good enough deputy if a man was hurt, and into goal I had to go. I have heard it said that "when England travelled abroad, they take two goalkeepers….the first choice and Hapgood." Be that as it may, I have several times deputised for an injured goalkeeper. My most vivid recollection was in 1935 at Goodison Park, Everton, when Moss was hurt in a vital League match. We didn't know at the time, but that injury was to lead to the finish of Frank's career.

Tom Whittaker and I helped him to the sidelines, and got his jersey off. And into goal I went. I was doing all right, and the other nine Arsenal players were keeping the ball away from me as much as possible, when, to a great cheer, Frank ran on to the field, wearing a spare Arsenal jersey, with his injured shoulder strapped up. Frank insisted in playing and the team was reshuffled with him at outside left. Frank was hurt again very soon, but to cap a gallant display, and just like the hero in a boys' story, he scored the equalising goal before he left the field for good. We went on to win the championship.

I have always said that had Frank been more fortunate, he would have, at least, been the equal of Harry Hibbs. But he had what is known to the medical profession as a recurring dislocation of the shoulder, and, although a Newcastle surgeon performed a marvellous operation on him by grafting a ligament from one part of his arm to the weak spot, Frank had to give up the playing side of the game after another accident at Blackburn a year later.

That match was responsible for my being 'sent off the field' for the only time in my career. I wasn't playing at the time, but sitting on a bench just inside the railings by the touchline with Mr. Allison. When Frank was hurt in throwing clear I ran on to the field to tell Leslie Compton to go into goal. Then I started to tell several other players to switch positions, but, before I could finish, the referee came up and ordered me from the field, which, of course, was quite in order. But things turned out all right and we won 1-0.

By the way I was once chosen to keep goal for England, but lost the chance at the last minute. We were playing Sweden at Stockholm, during the 1937 Scandinavian tour. I was travelling with the party but had not been chosen for the first game, against Norway at Oslo. During this match Vic Woodley, our goalkeeper, was hurt and it was thought he wouldn't be fit in time. So I was selected in his place, and, without wishing to deprive Vic of a cap, was secretly hoping to occupy this unique position. But Woodley recovered, and again I watched from the stand. I played in the last game of the tour, on what must be the world's worst football pitch, at Helsingfors (Finland). There were hoof mark and pot holes all over the pitch, and we were glad it was a bit of a canter.

84

Altogether, that ground was a terrific contrast to the luxury stadium we were to play in at Berlin the following year. Less than 15,000 Finns packed themselves in, and the stand, a band box compared to those on English grounds, held only 500 people. Among them, I remember, were the President, the Prime Minister and the Finland F.A. President, resplendent in top hat. But the prize for sartorial elegance went to the referee, who shone in the sun in a silk coat—and spats. We won that game 8-0, to make a total of eighteen goals for, none against, for the three matches. We beat Norway 6-0 and Sweden 4-0 in the previous games.

A few paragraphs ago I was talking about goalkeeping. Let me finish the chapter with a few references to my *goal-scoring* feats, if you can call them that. Actually, I can remember scoring only three times in top-class football. The first I got at Liverpool in a First Division game when I took a penalty. My shot was saved by Riley, but, following up, I headed the rebound into the net. The second I bagged at Southend in a wartime match for Arsenal when I ran through from our half to score what was described as a "brilliant goal after a great run!" And the other was for Chelsea in the first match of the 1944-45 season, against Fulham.

I nearly got another goal, but the only memory of that occasion was what Tom Whittaker has told me. It was against Everton and, half-an-hour from the end, I was involved in a crash and taken off for treatment. I recovered and went back onto the field, finishing the match at outside-left. But I don't remember that half-hour, even to this day. Tom Whittaker, however, saw it, and says, on one occasion, I ran through in real left-wing style, finishing with a shot which forced the goalkeeper to go full-length and turn the ball round the post!

CHAPTER 13

FILMS — AND HEAD-TENNIS

I was once told I was a 'natural' film star. Conveyor of this interesting information was a Polish girl named Jacie Rotawanda, who always popped up from nowhere and attached herself to Arsenal when we went on tour. She was mixed up in the film business as a sort of talent spotter, and after another meeting with her in Holland, I was inveigled into going along to see agents of Metro-Goldwyn-Mayer when we returned to London. They were quite interested, and so was Carl Brisson when we were introduced, but, eventually, advised me to stay in my own game. Which was what I had intended to do, anyway. But it was interesting while it lasted.

But I must tell you about the time when we nearly turned a Herbert Chapman training idea into a stage act. One of his introductions at Highbury had been what he called head-tennis. Played by three a-side on a tennis hard court, it was much the same as the game played on the sands of Continental resorts. The ball is played over the net either by head or feet, and only one bounce is allowed. The Arsenal lads got so excited when head-tennis came around during a training spell that Tom Whittaker was hard pressed to get us off the court. It is grand training, not only for the football, but for tennis, and, in fact any ball game.

Six of us, Ted Drake George Male, Leslie and Denis Compton, Cliff Bastin and myself, became so expert at head-tennis that Billy Blythe, the old Arsenal player, thought that the novelty, combined with our football names, might turn it into a stage act.

So, one morning, we went down to the Palladium, and gave a demonstration on the stage to Sir Oswald Stoll and George Black. Eddie Pola was the commentator and so well did the show go down that George Black made us a tentative offer of £100 a week between us.

In addition, we fixed up to make a tour of Butlin's Holiday Camps before we were to take the show on to the halls. But something went wrong, and, before the difficulties could be smoothed out, the new season was on us and the idea had to be temporarily dropped. Then, of course, the war came along to finish any idea I might have had of vying with Max Miller and Tommy Trinder as a top-liner at the Palladium. You never know where I might have finished….they say a comedian lives only for the day when he can play Hamlet!

Taken all round, we were quite a talented bunch at Highbury, at least from the sporting point of view. We could turn out a team at football, cricket, tennis, table tennis, golf, billiards or snooker, that would challenge anything put up by a similar organisation.

At one time, we had four county cricketers in Joe Hulme, Denis and Leslie Compton and Ted Drake, and a number of us were up to good club standard. We usually did very well in the "Evening News" Cricket Cup for footballers.

We all played golf. Frank Hill, Joe Hulme and Davie Jack were the best we had during my stay at Highbury, although in later years Alex James and Ted Drake wanted some beating off handicap. Joe Hulme was the billiard king and we used to have some tough snooker games.

Cards were, of course, the order of the day on away trips and during off-training moments, but I didn't get on very well, perhaps because of the unfortunate experience on the day I made my debut for Arsenal.

But I never reached the state one of the lads did on a train journey. The luck was going so badly against him in a 'brag' game that he opened the window of the carriage and threw the cards out! And it was our only pack.

CHAPTER 14

GRAND (DOLDER) HOTEL

A hotel I always remember as one of the loveliest spots I've ever seen was the Grand Dolder Hotel in Zurich. When the England party arrived there, after a fifteen hour trip from Berlin, it was just another hotel and we were glad to tumble into bed.

But next morning a look around showed us a delightful scene. The Grand Dolder is 1,900 feet above sea level and surrounded on three sides by beautiful gardens. In the grounds are a golf course round the lake, an open-air swimming pool, and ice-rink, tennis courts and a sun bathing lido. Altogether a fairy place, and I've promised myself a trip back there one of these days.

A humorous memory of the Grand Dolder is shared by Cliff Bastin and myself. Every mealtime during our stay at the hotel, when we arrived at the table, the rest of the players stood up, bowed, and with mock solemnity, chanted "Good morning, Arsenal." We never did find out whether they were pulling our legs, or just paying tribute to the League Championship Arsenal had pulled off again that season.

On the morning of the game we were taken to the Zoological Gardens in the Zurichberg and shown some of the rarest birds in captivity, white peacocks. After Switzerland had beaten us 2-1, one of the more superstitious of the party said that these queer birds had put a hoodoo on us!

I would put it down rather to the ground. It poured all the afternoon of the match, and, when we arrived, we found another match, a preliminary, being played on a pitch which was rapidly reaching a composite state of treacle and glue. Then they gave us a 'miniature' ball (Continental size) and sent us out to play. That match was all ruts, sliding tackles, and mud.

A similar sort of pitch greeted us at Prague when we played Czecho-Slovakia in 1934. But that was our fault.

We were taken to see the ground before the match. Large, very dry and dust covered. The Czech officials asked us anxiously if it was too dry and whether we would like it watered. We said O.K., a little wouldn't hurt and left the ground. Unfortunately, somebody misunderstood our suggestion, for they hosed on what looked like the entire municipal water supply. So that when we arrived to play, the pitch looked like a Transvaal trek trail, a combination of mud and dust.

A few paragraphs back I mentioned the superstition of the white peacocks in Zurich. I am not naturally addicted to this sort of fancy prophesying, but I had cause to think hard the following year when we lost to Yugo-Slavia in Belgrade, a match in which I was badly hurt.

Two days before the game when we were returning from a trip in Venice, we passed a funeral cortege on one of the famous waterways. The hearse and mourning coaches were specially constructed gondolas. On that occasion, I jokingly remarked, "It's always an unlucky sight to see a funeral before a match." But unlucky or not it's a sight you would only see in that unique, queer, city of Venice.

We went for several trips on the gondolas of Venice. I well remember my first outing, when, with some of the other players, I was gliding along in an ornate gondola in the moonlight. From one of the shuttered houses we caught the sound of a mandolin playing. It was pretty romantic, until I turned round, and saw hanging up in the back of the gondola, the tariff board! That spoilt it all. It was on that trip that we tried to make the gondolier break the speed limit. But he took a poor view of our repeated requests.

When we were off duty on our tours abroad, we were always looking for excitement. We found it all right in Rome when we hired two open, horse-drawn cabs, bribed the drivers to sit inside, then two of the lads clambered into the driving seats, and whipped up the horses to the fastest pace they had ever known. We went rattling through the streets of Rome in the greatest ride since Paul Revere. When the horses were exhausted, and the drivers nearly frantic with fear, we stopped the chariots and got well clear of the scene before the carabinieri arrived. Cliff Bastin and I were in the rear carriage which lost the race by a short head.

Another place I'm glad I saw in its original state was Ploesti, with its oil derricks and wells as far as the eye could see. It was an amazing sight, and, although my mind had not become attuned to the war which, even then, was fast approaching, I thought what a grand target it would make.

But my main memory of Ploesti was a humorous one. As captain of the English team, I was deputed to lay a wreath on the local war memorial. It shook me a bit when they showed me the wreath, which looked like a small florist's shop, and, worse still, we found out we had to walk nearly two miles up a hill before the wreath was to be laid. So I chose Stan Cullis to help me, and off we started at quite a fair pace with the band bringing up the rear. But it was hot, very hot, and half way up the hill we were definitely slowing. So much so that the band (how they played, and marched up that hill beat me) passed us almost at a gallop. And they were a good five lengths clear, and drawing away, by the time our objective was reached.

Mr. Winston Churchill greets the England team before the match with Scotland at Wembley, October, 1941.

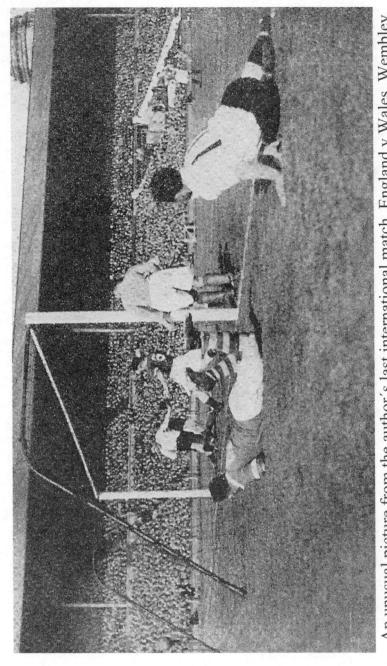

An unusual picture from the author's last international match, England v Wales, Wembley, February, 1943. Westcott (white shirt, in goalmouth) scores from a pass by Denis Compton (No. 11) who, with Dearson (No. 4) are both over the goal-line.

R.A.F. v Metropolitan Police, Wembley, 1942. Sir Philip Game inspects the R.A.F. team before the match.

A tense moment in the replayed War Cup Final at Preston. Collett (centre) watches anxiously as the author and Marks clear the ball from the goal-line.

Squadron Leader Tom Whittaker.

A picture which portrays the wizardry of Alex James. The three Manchester City players he has beaten with one swerve, watched with baffled faces as Alex moves on triumphantly towards goal.

Arsenal team conference. Mr. G. F. Allison demonstrates a move on the famous blackboard football pitch at Highbury. The author is on Mr. Allison's left.

This grand picture showing Arsenal's defensive plan for a corner was taken during the match with West Bromwich Albion at Highbury, 1938.

CHAPTER 15

FUSSBALLSPIELER

Arsenal once "lost" Alex James when we toured Germany and Sweden. It was after the ferry train, on the journey from Copenhagen to Hamburg, had been shunted on to the railway line, and moved off, that we discovered wee Alex was missing. But let Alex tell the story. I wish you could have been there when he told it for the first time.

"I had a nap on the ferry," said Alex, "and when I woke, found I was alone in Germany. I ran around shouting, 'Arsenal, Arsenal,' but, of course, nobody could understand me. (That's not surprising, considering Alex's terrific accent...). After a while, I took stock of myself, and found an English pound note in the pocket of my flannel bags. So I found a barber's and indicated I wanted a shave and a haircut. Then I went to a restaurant and saw in the rest of my money with my lunch and a drink. I was needing it then. After that I sat down on the ferry landing stage, to wait.

"After what seemed hours, the landing master came out of his office, called out something in German to me, and beckoned me into his office. I went in, and he was then talking on the phone. I heard him several times mention a word I took to be 'swindler,' but found out after he was saying Fussballspieler....footballer. Whoever was at the other end of the phone must have given him some instructions, for he wrote out on a label the words, "Alex James, Arsenal," tied it to my coat and bundled me on to a train. And imagine my relief when, some while later, the train drew into a station where the rest of Arsenal party were waiting for me."

Talk about nearly losing Alex. There was one trip when Arsenal nearly lost me. We were flying over to Paris to play the Racing Club and ran into thick fog. The plane I was in with some of the other players, including, I remember, little Bobby Davidson, was first away, and of course, as it was late afternoon when we took off, we knew nothing of the fog as we were crossing the Channel. But coming into Le Bourget, we (at least I) did begin to feel a little uneasy. The steward looked very worried, and the plane was flying in an uncertain manner. One of the lads asked the steward how long it would be before we landed, and he replied, "We are going down now, sir," rather after the fashion of Tommy Handley's Itma diver, who, of course, was not then in existence.

As he spoke, the plane dipped, then lurched, then went into a gentle dive, and everybody breathed a little easier. Suddenly, as we peered out of the windows, the engines roared, the nose lifted with a terrific jerk, and we saw the roof of a hangar flash past underneath the wing. The pilot, who was being brought in by beam, and who couldn't have known much more than us as to where we were, had come in too fast, and just managed to spot the hangar before we got there. As we sorted ourselves out again, after being thrown in a heap, he made another circuit of the landing field, and, this time, much to our relief, landed us safely somewhere out of the middle of fog-bound Le Bourget. He was a magnificent pilot, and only his cool head saved Arsenal from having to play about four men short the next afternoon.

If fate smiled on us in the air trip, she certainly gave us the thumbs down when we played the Racing Club that day. We had so many injuries and alterations that I'm not sure many of us knew what actually had happened until we read the papers next morning. In the first half Alf Kirchen pulled a muscle and Ernie Collett came on to replace him; Lewis came on after half-time and Ted Drake went to outside-right. And then Wilf Copping was hurt and Collett finished the match at left-half! In a game that seemed one long stoppage for injuries, perhaps the most unusual accident occurred to a Frenchman, the centre-half Jordan, who, ten minutes from the end, turned

100

a complete somersault, and laid himself out by striking his head with his own boot.

That air adventure was just one of the things that always seemed to be happening to me. I well remember that Scandinavian tour of 1937, to which I have referred to earlier. England nearly lost £100,000 worth of footballers in the fog. Travelling from Stockholm to Helsingfors for the Finland match, our ship was held up for twelve hours in the treacherous, rock-strewn water of the Finland Archipelago on the outward and return journeys. We had to anchor all night, which we thought was just as well, as our ship was only a 700-tonner. One scrape on those rocks and there wouldn't have been any more football for any of us. But the crowning blow was being turfed out of our beds at 7 a.m. for breakfast on the return journey although the boat hadn't moved an inch during the night.

It was while travelling with Arsenal that I was involved in two near train derailments. Coming back from Sheffield after a cup tie, the train took a sharp bend too fast, and, for a moment, everybody in our coach, at least I did, thought the train was going to turn over. We were dining at the time, and to a man, we got our soup all over us. Ted Drake complained of being dive-bombed by a couple of sticks of celery, but the only real casualty was Mr. Allison, who was badly bruised.

We were even luckier on the other occasion, going up to Wolverhampton for the opening match of 1939-40 season, our train ran over a piece of buckled rail near Coventry, and, for a few seconds, the coach danced up and down like a jeep with a wheel off. When we detrained at Wolverhampton, the guard told us we were lucky to be alive. We all agreed!

CHAPTER 16

A.C.₂ HAPGOOD (E.A.) R.A.F.

We had played four league games of that ill-fated 1939-40 season's programme when war came along to blow everything sideways. Like many another in our game, I was bewildered by it all and spent a few months trying to find out what was going to happen to soccer, and soccer players. During this time I was acting as a warden, and doing full-time duty. I naturally, saw some of the other Arsenal players, as our reporting post was in the Main Stand at Highbury Stadium. I well remember walking across the pitch in bright moonlight in the early hours one morning shortly after war was declared—and the sirens went. I've never crossed the ground so fast in my life either before or since.

In our spare time we fixed up a few games of football and Tom Whittaker, our trainer, who played for Arsenal after serving in the last war, scored five goals in one match.

Then I joined the Air Force, and found myself in an entirely new life. Gone was the Eddie Hapgood, Arsenal and England captain, and, in his place, A.C. 'two plonks' Hapgood, E.A., who, to authority, was just another 'Erk.'

Going into the Services for the first time got me just like it affected thousands of others. Frankly, I admit I was very fed up at the change in my life, and I revolted at being treated as if I were a head of cattle, or a sheep, or just like nothing at all. Later on I laughed at myself, but, in the beginning, I was very miserable.

I reported at Cardington for my first day in the Air Force. The Battle of Britain was fast approaching, but I didn't feel like one of the Few. With seventeen others, I was assigned to a hut and given directions by a matter-of-fact

Corporal, to whom eighteen recruits were just another bunch of civilians to be knocked into shape as airmen.

During the roll-call he reached my name, "Hapgood, E.A.—any relation to the Arsenal player?" he barked. "The same," I said, rather self-consciously. "Oh-ho," he smiled, or rather, as I thought, leered. "Well, you played for a classy team, we'll give you a classy job. Just get down and polish this floor." With that he pitched a tin of polish at me. Instinctively, I trapped the tin as it skidded across the floor at me.... and banged it back, left foot, at him! Well, that was a bad start, but I weathered that storm all right. Afterwards, I found out the Corporal was a Tottenham fan, but not a bad bloke for all that.

The next day I started to look around a bit, and, after a stroll around the camp, lay down on the grass in the sunshine and watched the world go by. Idly I browsed, and, in the distance, saw a man struggling along with a terrible limp, dragging his leg and looking very miserable. As he got nearer I heard a voice shout in an unmistakable and familiar Gaelic accent "Eddie Hapgood, the first Christian face I've seen for weeks."

It was Billy Shankley, Preston half-back and an old opponent on the international field. Billy had a bad toe, was generally browned-off, but ready, as usual, to talk 'fitba.' So was I, for that matter, and we yearned away about the 'good old days' until the Sergeant came and broke it up with 'On parade, everybody.'

I shall never forget my stay at Cardington. Three weeks later I was taken to the R.A..F. sick bay with multiple septic whitlows on both hands and spent the next two-and-a-half months there undergoing operations.

While I was in hospital I read that I had been chosen for an R.A.F. representative side the following week. Of course, I couldn't play, and was I fed up! Later, of course, I played fairly often for the Service side.

Hospital treatment over, I moved on to Cosford for a course as a P.T. instructor, during which I had to go over a battle course of a mile in sixteen minutes, carrying full kit. Fit as I was it was a bit of an ordeal, and as I staggered up to the finishing line, inside the time limit I am glad to say, but only just, the checking officer said "Nice work, Hapgood, now run along and have a bath".

The 'run along' was rich. I had finished on my knees anyway....and when I got to the 'bath,' it was a bowl of icy cold water. But I don't suppose it did me any harm, for all that.

From Cosford I moved, a fully qualified P.T. Corporal, to Ruislip, arriving there late one winter's afternoon, very wet, heavily laden, and, need I add, browned off.

At the guard room, they told me politely, there was no accommodation for me at the moment, but that something would be fixed up for the night, and I'd have to straighten things up for myself in the morning. Then the S.P. called on a Corporal Radcliffe to show me to some temporary sleeping quarters. With Radcliffe carrying a pile of blankets, and me still loaded with kit, we ploughed through the rain, past huts, barracks and outbuildings for what seemed miles, each moment getting more miserable.

We passed one sleeping hut with a young Erk learning out of the window. Spotting me, he called out, "Is that Eddie Hapgood?" I wasn't very interested, but replied it was. "I'm Sibley, of Southend," he replied. With which my escorting corporal threw down the blankets into a nice healthy looking puddle and, in a broad Lancashire accent, shouted, "Well, what do you know. I'm Radcliffe, of Oldham Athletic." Things weren't so bad after all; I was among friends again.

I'm not going to give away anybody by stating the name of the camp at which the following incident happened, but early in my R.A.F. life I was involved one of the queerest happenings it has every been my lot to encounter.

I was in trouble again. Not that I was a bad 'soldier.' Rather, it was hard to learn all the little differences between civilian and Service life. What I was charged with I didn't really know, but I was confined to barracks—on a Saturday morning a few hours before I was due to play for Arsenal against Tottenham at White Hart Lane.

I asked the sergeant who was 'in charge' of me, couldn't something be done about it, and vaguely muttered something about parole. He explained, at great length, what being on a charge meant, and also that being confined to barracks didn't mean being allowed to travel outside to play football! But I wasn't satisfied, and asked if I might see the duty officer. At last, my request was granted and I was ushered into his presence.

Naturally, he wasn't very interested in my request for a few hours' leave that afternoon, but when I explained I didn't know what I was charged with, he said, "You are doing it now!"

Then he explained, you don't use your hands to emphasise points when answering an officer, and you don't rest your hands on the table when you are talking to an officer, and that you stand to ATTENTION when talking to an officer. The last in a firm tone, which left no doubt in my mind I had been doing wrong.

I apologised, explaining my ignorance of Service rules, etc., that I always talked like that anyway, and I would very much like a few hours off. He was a sport and said, "If you promise to go to the match under escort, I'll let you out this afternoon." Thinking, of course, I'd refuse. I jumped at the idea, and, before he could retract his permission, had saluted and was away.

Later, two warrant-officers presented themselves at the guard-room, and I was led away to a Service car in which we all drove to Tottenham. At the gate I 'vouched' for my two 'friends,' who, by this time were also seeing the funny side of

105

the situation. But they did their duty. They accompanied me to the dressing-room, sat either side of me while I changed (anybody looking in on that room would have thought Arsenal were going to field thirteen men that afternoon), and ignored the remarks of the other lads, who actually didn't know what it was all about.

My two shadows were on either side when I picked up the ball to lead Arsenal on to the field. And they only left me at the end of the tunnel on the touchline.

They were there at half-time, and again at the finish. After the match, I dressed in record time, and we all left for the drive back to the airfield. Which must be the only occasion anybody has ever played in a professional football match under open arrest.

I might add the charge against me was dismissed on the following Monday.

Taken all round I enjoyed life as an N.C.O. in the R.A.F. The main idea was that you had to buckle down and make a go of it, or be miserable for the rest of your Service life. I made a host of new friends and got involved in many arguments concerning professional football on, and off, the field. Soccer is a universal discussion point in any and all of the Services, and, frequently, at our meal table we had lads arguing for, or against, very nearly every professional club in the country. As well as Scots, Irishmen and the little old Welsh, look you, who argued as they played, with fervour.

One fellow, a staunch Newcastle supporter, we voted the job of tea-taster at Ruislip. At breakfast each morning he had to take a sip from each of the three urns before deciding which was tea, coffee or cocoa!

Before taking my commission, I visited a fair number of camps, and nearly always managed to fit in a game of soccer with the local club. They made me captain of West Bromwich when I was stationed in the Midlands, I played for Lovells when on a course at the giant R.A.F. camp at St.

Athans, and was given permission by Arsenal to play for Luton when posted to a Bedfordshire station in the full glory of a Pilot-Officer's rank.

Although we lost more games than we won, I had a lot of fun playing for Luton. They were a hard-working bunch of youngsters, and the club has an enthusiastic Board. Perhaps some of the players got discouraged when a goal or two down—you never got that with Arsenal in the old days—but I think there's the makings of a good club at Luton after the war.

We never got many of the breaks. Losing clubs like Orient will tell you how badly the ball runs for you when the luck is out, and, in one game, against Chelsea, we should have been four goals up in the first ten minutes before Joe Payne found his scoring boots against his old club. We lost 6-0.

And I remember the Tottenham match when Rowley, the Manchester United forward, scored seven against us at White Hart Lane. Two critics summed that game up as 'Luton had as much of the play as Spurs, but Rowley could do nothing wrong!' Just one of those things, anyway.

But I am straying from the point. Things didn't happen to me in the same way when I got a commission as they had in the ranks. I had come a long way, and had learnt a lot.

Perhaps my brightest memory as an officer was one night making the rounds as duty officer, I was hailed by a prisoner in the guard-room, "Hullo Eddie, when are you going to play for Arsenal again?" I passed that incident over with all the dignity I could muster....but secretly thought, "Well, the old club supporters haven't forgotten me, after all."

CHAPTER 17

WARTIME SOCCER

Perhaps the game I remember most of all in wartime was, the 1941 Cup Final at Wembley, when we drew 1-1. Or, rather, what happened afterwards. The game, itself, was anybody's after Les Compton had hit the Preston post from a penalty after six minutes, and his brother, Denis, gave us the equaliser after Preston scored first.

But that night I stayed in town instead of going back to my R.A.F. camp, and the Germans launched their heaviest air raid of the war on London. It was a terrific business, and perhaps the heaviest raid made by either side until the R.A.F. introduced their 1,000 bomber raids to the cowering people of Cologne. I came to the conclusion, as I lay and listened to the crashing of the mighty barrage and the whistle of falling bombs, that I didn't like air raids, and never would.

Wartime football was, taken all round, a queer experience. Several matches were interrupted by sirens, while after I joined the R.A.F., I never really knew from one week's end to another for whom I would be playing on the following Saturday. Representative matches were usually all right, for I could always fix my duties accordingly, but when I was posted it wasn't always easy to get a weekly game.

There was the time when I was at Cosford on my commission course, and West Bromwich asked me to play, and also, whether I could find another good full-back at the R.A.F. camp. I could, and did—it was Laurie Scott, my Arsenal colleague. We played, and helped West Bromwich to beat Birmingham at the Hawthorns.

Sometimes, of course, we were short, and, here, the guest player (which I was to other clubs on several occasions) helped out. But Arsenal tried, if possible, always to field their own players before seeking the help of outsiders. I kept goal for Arsenal in a wartime match because we were short-handed. George Marks had not put in an appearance, and Mr. Allison told me to put his green jersey on.

It was a cup-tie with Tottenham, and, naturally, with both clubs playing on their 'home' ground (Arsenal used White Hart Lane during wartime), I came in for a bit of chipping. On one occasion, when we were pressing, I walked some distance out of my goal, only to hear the sally, "Take your goal with you, Eddie"....which made me scuttle back hurriedly. We drew 1-1, the first time I had ever been beaten while keeping goal!

Mr. Allison's difficulties weren't made any easier as regards wartime matches when representative games were afoot. Arsenal players were always in demand, and, on one afternoon, he had to find substitutes for seven players, involved in two different games, but not free to refuse and play for their club. George Marks, Bernard Joy, Ted Drake, Alf Kirchen and I were chosen for the R.A.F. at Newcastle, and Swindin and Bryn Jones for the Ack-Ack X1 against the South-Eastern Command at Reading. Incidentally, Alex James nearly made a come-back in that match. He was chosen to stand by to play for the Ack-Ack if Bryn Jones couldn't get up from South Wales. But Bryn made the date all right, and Alex watched from the stand.

One of the hardest games I had during wartime was in Bristol, my old home town. It was a nice gesture of the Football Association to ask me to captain their team against the Royal Air Force in Bristol's first big game of the war. Poor old Bristol had been badly hit in the blitzes, but that didn't stop the soccer fans from rolling along to Ashton Gate to see the match. My mother was there, and also old-time stars Billy Wedlock and Harold Fleming.

I was matched against my old rival, Stan Matthews, but he dropped out at the last minute, and, in his place, I got the 'nightmare' wing of the quicksilver Leslie Smith, and twinkle-toed Irish Alex Stevenson. They made me cover plenty of territory that day, for both were in superb form. I think I would have preferred Stan Matthews after all— he doesn't run so fast as Les Smith!

The F.A. goalkeeper was Brown, the young Queens Park goalkeeper, who kept a good goal, although we lost 4-2. He's a promising lad, and I particularly liked his modest bearing. After another representative game we played in, at Luton, he came up to me after he had let in one tricky shot, and had made some other very good saves, and said he thought he had played a bad game. I told him he hadn't and added, "Don't ever say what you think about your game…let others do that for you." Always a good piece of advice to a goalkeeper, I think.

Young Reg Lewis, who was just finding his feet in the Arsenal side in 1939, made great strides in wartime football. He is a brilliant ball player. Lewis had the unusual experience of playing for the R.A.F. after being selected as twelfth man for the Army. It happened at Ayr, and when the sides mustered for the big representative match, it was found the R.A.F. were one short, so Major Sloan, genial Army soccer secretary, immediately offered his opposite number, Squadron-Leader Jimmy Jewell, the services of Lewis.

Perhaps Lewis's best wartime game was in the 1943 Final against Charlton. I wasn't playing that day, so had the opportunity of watching the lad in action. He got four smash-hit goals, the last of which couldn't have been bettered by the great G. O. Smith.

Another Arsenal player, who was helped by the less-boisterous nature of wartime football, was Denis Compton, who steadily, but surely, built himself up a reputation as a great left-winger. He is a deadly shot with his left foot, and often, slapped one in with what is known as his 'dummy,' his right foot, thought by many to be useless as a scoring weapon.

I remember one game, at Brighton, when Denis came straight from a battle course and then proceeded to chase about to every part of the Brighton ground. I have never seen so much energy. He got a couple of goals as well, one from a penalty. But Denis was glad to sit down in the dressing-room after the game. As he remarked, hauling Bren guns in the early hours of the morning doesn't make it any easier to play football!!

Denis's brother, Leslie, elder Compton, had some mixed experiences. In the early days of the war, Les, normally a full-back, was pressed into service as the Arsenal centre-forward... and, immediately, started scoring goals in Dixie Dean style. He got six against Clapton Orient in one game, and in the Inter-Allied Services Cup Final, at Stamford Bridge, scored five of the six goals by which the Police beat the Army.

It was Les who took my place in the England team immediately after I had broken the international record, and, although he lost his place, regained it before the end of the next season. One game he played in for us sticks in my mind. It was against Charlton at the Valley very early in the war and the top-surface of the pitch was a mixture of melted snow, mud, treacle and glue! At least, that's how it seemed to us. The game was a high-speed thriller run over in slow motion. You had to think hard before making a move in case you couldn't recover your footing. Les's long loping stride seemed to suit itself on that surface, and he got a couple of hard-hit goals.

Early in the war Arsenal set up a unique record, by fielding an entire team of men serving in the Royal Air Force. And, strangely enough, there were still enough top-class players left in the R.A.F. for them to turn out a representative side against us at Tottenham. Our team was: Boulton (a former Arsenal player who left us just before the war to join Derby County); Scott, Hapgood; Crayston, Bernard Joy, Male;

111

Kirchen, Drury, Drake, Curtis, Leslie Jones. We drew that match 1-1.

I had some good games with the R.A.F., whom I led until injury forced me to drop out in the dressing-room a few minutes before the side took the field against Scotland at Newcastle. In one match, against Hibs at Edinburgh, I had my first glimpse of young Gordon Smith, for whom many experts predict a great future. He's good, fast, rather like Alex Jackson in his prime, and I think Scotland, if they give him the right inside-forward, have found a winner.

In the majority of R.A.F. teams I played for, George Marks was the goalkeeper. He has been a bit unlucky through injuries, some of which have happened through his own impetuosity, and others through the normal accidents which seem to occur to the more adventurous type of goalkeeper. Marks is, of course, an Arsenal player, and came right to the fore a few months before war broke. He was signed from Salisbury Corinthians, and after a spell with Enfield and Margate, our two nursery teams, he had his first senior game in a friendly against Ipswich. And then, chosen as reserve goalkeeper for our Continental tour at the end of the 1938-39 season, he travelled as first team goalkeeper owing to Swindin being kept back in England through injury. Marks is a good goalkeeper, very daring, with safe hands and is a long kicker.

Internationals in the early days of the war were strange compared with peacetime games. But they were a grand tonic for the public, and, after all, we were lucky to be able to play any football at all. While the B.E.F. was battling its way back to the beaches and Dunkirk, we travelled north for a charity international with Scotland, for which the police had allowed only a 70,000 limit. Actually, there was only about 61,000 when we took the field, and Hampden Park was more or less deserted, with the barrage balloons over Clydebank looking like birds in the distance.

A few hours before the match, we were without a goalkeeper. Sam Bartram had his R.A.F. leave cancelled, and we were told Vic Woodley was somewhere on his way from the South. He turned up, thus saving me the job of keeping goal! It was as well Vic arrived, as we had a tough match and only managed to hold the ancient enemy to a 1-1 draw.

A couple of weeks before that, we played host to Wales, playing their first game at Wembley. And all things considered, it was rather wonderful that nearly 50,000 turned up for that match. We lost by the only goal, a long shot from Bryn Jones twisting out of Sam Bartram's hands. No wonder they call Wembley the goalkeeper's graveyard. Wales, as usual, found the man for the occasion that day. With Tom Jones unable to travel, magician Ted Robbins pulled Bob Davies, the Notts Forest centre-half, out of the hat. And he stole the match for Wales. I think that Wales should definitely be given a Wembley Saturday game after the war.

Another outstanding match with Wales was at bomb-scarred St. Andrews, which has been probably the most damaged ground in the country. We beat them that day, thanks to goals from Jimmy Hagan and Maurice Edelston. Poor Harry Goslin, Bolton captain who was one of the first professional footballers to be called up, and who went through Dunkirk before losing his life in the Middle East, played for England and played well. He always did that. There were plenty of Arsenal players in that match too….Denis Compton, George Marks and myself on the English side, Leslie Jones and Horace Cumner for Wales.

Cumner had one good match against us a little later when his two goals were one too many for England at Wolverhampton. At one time, it was feared Cumner would never play football again, for he was terribly burnt in an accident while serving in the Royal Marines. But I am glad to say he recovered fully and will, I think, be the first choice for Wales at outside-left for many years to come.

113

The Royal Box was nearly always crowded when we played a charity international at Wembley during the war. At one match there were seven Cabinet Ministers present.... Sir James Grigg, Mr. A.V.Alexander, Lord Woolton, Lord Leathers, Mr. Herbert Morrison, Mr. Ernest Bevin and Mr. Clement Attlee.

Perhaps the most exciting of all internationals I played in during the war was the 1942 clash at Hampden, with Scotland. Nine goals were scored that day, and the five that Scotland got were the highest ever totalled against an England side for which I played in 33 games. Two memories of that game—young Gordon Bremner, yet another Arsenal 'find,' making a grand debut for Scotland, and Joe Mercer calling himself 'One-eyed Joe' after getting the ball in his face early in the game. My old friend Bill Shankley, nearly went crazy when he scored the winning goal for Scotland. Billy is soccer mad, particularly where Scotland is concerned.

I had two outstanding incidents with Chelsea, or, perhaps, I should say three. I played half-back in two Christmas games against them, because we were short of middle men, and we lost both games 2-5 and 1-5. It was a bit tough on the first occasion, the Christmas Day, that Denis Compton, Alf Kirchen, Bernard Joy sat in the stand and watched us lose because they were under orders not to play for Arsenal, as they might have tired themselves for the big Service games at Leeds the following day. Later in the war I played for Chelsea against a star-studded Aldershot side at Stamford Bridge, and we won 8-0. There must be a moral there somewhere!

Brentford were always a bogey in wartime games. They, in fact, became a regular hoodoo. In one Cup semi-final at Tottenham in May, 1942, we won the game from pillar to post, and yet Brentford passed on to meet Portsmouth in the Final. Even Brentford supporters admitted they were lucky and that's saying a lot. But it was a thriller. When Douglas

114

Hunt scored to make it 2-1 five minutes from time, we were not only unlucky, but out of the Cup. But straight from the kick-off Reg Lewis raced through, and, when only a few yards from goal, was brought down. A penalty was immediately awarded, and the only two cool men on the field were Johnny Jackson, Chelsea's international keeper, on loan to Brentford, and Cliff Bastin, who was to take the kick. But, for once, Cliff's magic boots failed him, and Jackson saved the point blank shot.

Wartime also brought a renewal of that time-honoured match, Amateurs and Professionals, after a ten years' absence from the lists. This game, in February, 1940, was played at Selhurst Park, with snow underfoot. Not the best of surfaces, but a good time was had by all. Strangely enough, the amateurs weren't numbered while we wore a spare set of Crystal Palace jerseys with the numbers prominently displayed.

Len Goulden got a grand goal in that match. It was worked out almost by the board and set square. He sent Leslie Smith away down the left wing, sauntered into the goalmouth, marked his position (any minute I expected to see him brush his hair) and leisurely headed the return into the net. It looked so easy nobody congratulated him.

I played a number of games for the Football League side, including a star-studded match with the All-British XI at Wolverhampton on the first Boxing Day of the war, when the conditions were just about as awful as I have ever seen them. In that game we had the first instance of what was to become common practice during the war of playing a substitute. Stan Cullis was held up on his way from Aldershot, and the former Wolves player who went to Rochdale, Rhodes, held the fort until his arrival.

To conclude this necessarily abbreviated chapter on wartime football, I append a story of Tommy Walker, one of the greatest inside forwards Scotland ever produced, a gentlemanly type of player, who, after the war is to go into the church, and a man it is a delight to know and to play against. The match I am writing about included neither Tommy nor I, but, nevertheless, the great hearted Hearts player was a "material" factor in it.

The Scottish F.A., running short of equipment a few days before the Hampden match with England in April, 1943 sent out an S.O.S. for international jerseys and stockings with the proviso that, should the kit be used, they would replace it after the war. Tommy Walker was one of the first to offer his collection—a matter of seventeen jerseys. And so, although he wasn't selected for the match, ten of the players wore the jerseys he had carried to fame against the national "enemy."

Willie Buchan, who came into the side for Tommy, was clad in the jersey worn by Walker when he netted that historic penalty which won for Scotland the international trophy in the first year of its existence—the penalty I gave away at Wembley! Jock Dodds had the inspiration of the dark blue shirt worn by Walker when Tommy scored two story-book goals against Wales at Tynecastle, and turned apparent defeat into magnificent victory.

Alec Venters used the shirt in which Tommy once went through the complete English defence to score a magnificent goal at Wembley; and Waddell sported the jersey that Walker played in what he has described as his best international—against Ireland at Belfast, when he partnered Jimmy Delaney of Celtic, and formed a right-wing that was compared to the Wembley wizard pair, Alec Jackson and Tim Dunn. The match should go down into history as the "Walker 'National." Sad to relate the Scots lost 4-0.

CHAPTER 18

BACKSTAGE HIGHBURY

"With the full knowledge that this will start something, I would like to put forward the opinion that if the Arsenal slip far enough to be in danger of relegation, a happening approaching disaster will have occurred in British football....the Arsenal are more than a soccer club—they are an institution."

TREVOR WIGNALL,
Daily Express, 16th Nov., 1937.

The purpose of my book was to set down (for posterity?) something of my football life, but, as my career was so intimately connected with Arsenal, I feel it would not be out of place if I devote the next few pages to Highbury as it affected me.

There was an atmosphere about backstage Arsenal, which I venture to say, was its very own. Even now, after being away from the Stadium for over five years—except for occasional visits—I can reach back into the past and get that grand old feeling. I was particularly sensitive to it, being chock-full of self-confidence myself. There was a feeling, that, once you put on an Arsenal shirt, nothing could go wrong, that your team was better than all the others. Arsenal atmosphere it was called by those on the outside, but we knew it was team spirit, an indefinable something which carried us to the heights, kept us there, and which won us games that, by all the laws and rights, we should have lost. Lucky we were called at times, many times.

Perhaps we were on the odd occasion, but we never forgot that great though a player might me in an individual position, he was useless if the others weren't on the field with him. Jack Crayston summed it up best when he once likened Arsenal to the parable of the sticks. Singly, he quoted, we can be broken down, together nothing can break us. It may have been an oblique hint to a youngster who hadn't quite assimilated the Arsenal atmosphere, but it certainly was very true.

Chapman started that team spirit in his own wizard way, and it has been fostered since his death by Mr. Allison and all connected with the playing side of the team. Dirty play or shady tricks are not tolerated. We went out to play the game, and if we lost, well that was too bad, but next week we would do better. The team conferences helped us to understand the special difficulties connected with playing positions other than our own, and, at the same time, helped us to find the weak spots in the opposition armour. Not very often did a player fail to fit in with the Arsenal methods. If it was impossible to train him our way, then he left Highbury. But that seldom happened.

The majority of the players felt, as did I, the honour of playing for Arsenal. In later years I shall miss the thrill of wearing the red and white shirt which was carried to so much honour and glory during the time I spent in North London.

As I say, Chapman started it all. He humoured us, even kidded us (I know he did with me, and Alex James will tell you the same about himself). He was a human dynamo himself, but he knew just how far to drive us. If he wanted us to grasp a certain point in an argument he was trying to put over, off would come his coat, and, using arms and legs to the danger of any unwary object which might be in the way, he would demonstrate exactly what he meant. In one such demonstration he smashed a hat and a coat stand without, apparently, noticing the damage.

It is rather hard to try and get over to you readers what I mean about Arsenal, because, of course, I was one of them, and, in some way, it sounds like personal boasting. But we were proud of ourselves, as I suppose we were entitled to be.

I'd like you to have a look round backstage Arsenal, as I knew it before the war, so here goes for a conducted tour of what, to the majority of people, is a realm as closely guarded as a Tibetan Monastery.

We enter the Main Stand in Avenall Road, being passed in by the commissionaire at the two big swing doors, on which are embossed the Arsenal initials. Directly facing the entrance, on the far side of the Memorial Hall, and in a little recess, is a dominating bronze bust of Herbert Chapman, who never lived to see the giant stand erected but who silently watches over Arsenal's fortunes.

To the left, just inside the entrance, is the enquiry office. Beyond that, a corridor, along which we proceed after climbing a few steps. The first door is marked 'Referee Only.' A peep inside shows us a neat little room, complete with bath. Next door is an interesting room, occupied on match days by the band, already tuning up for their performance before and during the coming game. They are members of the Highgate Silver Band, but were always known as the Arsenal Band.

Back along the corridor, we pass a door opposite the referee's room, which is his private entrance to the pitch. Across the hall, past the Chapman bust, and through another door we come to the playing side of the organisation. On the left, as we go through, are store rooms, where supplies of equipment of all descriptions are kept. To the right, inside the first door is the Visitors' Dressing Room, with baths. Slightly different in shape from our room, it is roughly the same size. We won't stay here long, but have a closer look at the Home Dressing Room when we get there. Next along the passage is the Trainers' Office, where Tom Whittaker and Billy Milne hold sway. Then the treatment room, fitted to the last degree with modern electrical apparatus. I've spent many a happy (?) hour in this room with Tom, coat off and bustling about busily, treating his 'patients' in turn. Surprising how many casualties three teams can produce between them on a Saturday.

119

Passing rapidly on, we have now reached the Home Team Dressing Room. One of the largest I have ever been in on a League ground, it is fitted down to the last detail for the players' comfort. A bench runs round three sides of the room, which is tiled from the ceiling to halfway down the wall. Above the benches hang clothes pegs, numbered in order of position. No. 1 peg starts the order on the far side of the room, nearest the baths. That is used by the goalkeeper, and the others run in sequence, right-back, left-back, and so on. Over on the fourth side of the room is a recess containing a rubbing table, where we had a last-minute massage before turning out.

A section of the floor, running the distance of the benches, is steam-heated. No, not because we were cotton-wool footballers, but you cannot play with cold feet, and no chance was taken of a shock to our system when we put our bare feet on the floor while changing from outdoor kit to football gear. The new House of Commons is to have this system.

Incidentally, some players, took a long time to get changed. They were the ones who took every precaution in order to cut down the risk of injury. Some, of course, overdid things—there were those who used plentiful doses of vaseline inside or outside their socks, ankle bandages, cotton-wool below the bottom of their shin-pads, knee supports and other accessories. I never wore knee or ankle bandages and I don't see they are necessary unless, of course, ordered medically. The majority of us always had a pre-match massage from Tom and a rubbing of eucalyptus oil, very warming on cold days.

But I am digressing again. On we go through the door behind the goalkeeper's seat. To the left is the boot room, with our boots hanging in pairs in neat array. There was no special allotment of boots a season. A player hung on to his old pair until he felt it necessary to break in a new set....which, he did, usually, in the garden or on the allotment! Apropos of this

120

room....we actually travelled with our own cobbler on away trips. On we go, and are now in the bathroom. On the left are four showers, then the cold bath, with the hot bath (known to the lads as "Littlewoods," a pool capable of holding the entire team at once) completing the rest of that side of the room. To our right are hand basins, then a chromium massage bath, two small single baths, and, finally, the foam bath....which we all enjoyed using.

Back to the dressing-room, and across the corridor, through a door on the right, down a few steps to the left, a right hand turn and down the tunnel to the pitch. At the bottom, almost on the touchline, is a two-sided shelter, covered by glass. On either side are four seats, above them a notice, "Trainers' seats, and one reserve." At the side of the right-hand seats is a phone attachment connected directly to the Board Room. If Mr. Allison wished to make a positional change during the match or if he had any other orders to pass on to Tom Whittaker, it was easy for him to nip out of his seat in the Directors' Box and make his wishes known.

Retracing our path back along the tunnel to the Main Hall, we take the staircase immediately to the right of the doorway. To the left, at the top, first door along the corridor, are the directors' and ladies' retiring rooms, and, beyond them, the Press Room. The newspaper lads have their own passage-way through to their seats.

On the other side from the staircase is Mr. Allison's office. I had good cause to remember this room. It's not very large, but there's quite a bit of stuff crammed in....a bookcase, a largish desk, crowded, and yet always tidy. To Mr. Allison's right is a large grandfather clock, presented to Arsenal by the London Combination. Behind him, on the wall above the mantelshelf, an animal's head (it looked like a weasel or a stoat) with the inscription, 'to G. F. Allison, from Ilfracombe Football Club.' Hanging on the nose is a banner, a relic of a Continental tour. There are also a few souvenirs occupying places on the mantelpiece. On a little side table to Mr. Allison's left are two phones, one a house phone connecting to all parts of the Stadium.

Leaving the Manager's Office, we make our way along to the Board Room. Spacious, it has panelled walls, green-backed leather chairs, and a large conference table. The decorations throughout are walnut. There are ten chairs, nine of them carrying the Arsenal initials on the leather upholstery. On the front of the Chairman's high-backed chair is a field gun embossed in gold, the Arsenal emblem.

Next is the gymnasium, where I spent quite a lot of time, and always enjoyed using. It is about sixty feet long, and fitted with everything guaranteed to keep the lads occupied in their task of getting one hundred per cent fit. There are rowing machines, head-balls, punch-balls, trapeze bars and rings, and the rest. At the far end of the gym is the washing room, its main piece of furniture being an electric washing machine. Here was cleaned up all our training kit... our match equipment was, of course, sent weekly to the laundry. There is also a drying room handy. Novel innovation here are the stocking stretchers. Billy Milne always said if our stockings were sent to the laundry, they'd come back shrunk to the size of a pair of gloves.

Incidentally, it may be interesting to know that our jerseys cost a guinea each, and we usually got through at least four sets a peacetime season. As a point of interest, the new red shirts with white sleeves were first shown to the public on March 4, 1933, when we played Liverpool at Highbury. Unfortunately, they didn't bring us much luck that day, because we lost1-0. I still remember the amazed whistles from the crowd, when we ran out in our new finery. And, also, when we wore the red-and-white hooped stockings (later changed to blue-and-white hoops) for the first time. They were both Chapman brain waves, to help us spot each other in a hurry during a match. Surprising how many teams copied the hooped-stockings idea.

But I am digressing yet again. Let's go out into the stand and have a final view from way up here, especially if you are in the select company allowed into the Directors' Box. Here in the front row, are four seats still bearing the name of the late Earl of Lonsdale, our former President. Mr. Allison's seat is in the back row, near the entrance. In the front, to the centre, are a number of seats reserved for Royalty, or other particularly distinguished guests. Around, above and below, stretches the bulk of this giant double-decker, one of the most carefully-planned on any ground in the country, and which cost £100,000 to erect.

Among other innovations, and there is very little lacking, are broadcasting and television boxes, a workshop and office for our own Clerk of the Works, who has permanent residence on the ground, separate first-aid rooms for men and women, a giant horseshoe-shaped bar at the top of the stand—98 feet long, and the second largest in the world—and a microphone room, one of the instruments being used for police control of the ground. They were first used, I believe, for our annual mid-week game with Glasgow Rangers in 1936. It was after one of these games with Glasgow Rangers, by the way, that we signed Doctor Marshall. His goal, a grand effort, created a great impression. Doc Marshall was always more interested in his profession than in soccer, and the last I heard of him was that he had obtained a Council medical post in an East London suburb.

Coming back to the present from our imaginary tour of peacetime Highbury, I must say the ground has been very lucky to have received only comparatively light damage from enemy action during the time it has been under Government control (it was taken over at the beginning of the war). The covered enclosure behind the North-West goal was completely demolished one night in the big blitz. Billy Milne,

123

our assistant-trainer, who did a 24-hour on and 24-hour off warden duty on the ground all through the war, tells me 124 incendiaries dropped on the ground alone that night, and one of the minor comedies of the action was the sight of the goalposts burning merrily. Also an H.E. smashed the concrete terracing at the other end to the right of the clock. Luckily, apart from a few chairs burned away by incendiaries, the lucky double-decker stands are intact. So the old place won't have changed very much when they run out for the first peacetime match.

Incidentally, to close this chapter, here are two diverse instances of the thoroughness and care of detail in which things were done at Highbury.

No risks were ever taken when we were travelling abroad, either to the players or to a possible loss of the playing strength. A particular instance was the 1936 F.A. Continental tour, when six of the Cup-winning side (Bastin, Bowden, Copping, Crayston, Male and myself) as well as Tom Whittaker, were chosen to travel. Arsenal insured the bunch of us for £56,000 (£8,000 each) additional cover to that already taken out by the F.A.

The other story concerns nearly £100,000 spent by the club on players' transfers over a period of ten years. Here's how the money went:

Bryn Jones (from Wolves, 1938) £14,000; David Jack (Bolton, 1928) £10,890; Alex James (Preston, 1929) £9,000; Jimmy Dunne (Sheffield United, 1933) £8,250; Ernie Coleman (Grimsby Town, 1932) £8,000; Wilf Copping (Leeds, 1934) £8,000; Dave Halliday (Sunderland, 1929) £6,500; Ted Drake (Southampton, 1934) £6,000; Alf Kirchen (Norwich City, 1935) £6,000; Jackie Milne (Blackburn Rovers, 1935) £5,000; and, Bobby Davidson (St. Johnstone, 1935) £4,000. Then, of course, there were players like Dr. Marshall, Bowden, Crayston and Moss, who didn't come for nothing.

CHAPTER 19

PREPARATION FOR VICTORY

As I have previously written, I did most of my training on my own, but, of course, was subject to club discipline like anybody else. A résumé of normal training procedure at Highbury will give some idea of what we did during the week to fit ourselves for the Saturday game.

Contrary to popular belief, a football ground is usually busy on a Sunday. It is treatment day. Anybody hurt in the Saturday's games (we ran three teams), turned up for attention from Tom and Billy Milne. One Sunday during the 1937-38 season, "Doc" Whittaker treated thirteen 'patients' —Copping, Crayston, Les Compton, Roberts, Kirchen, Collett, Hulme, Bob John, Scott, Atter, Pryde, Carr and myself!

When I first arrived at Highbury, training didn't really commence until Tuesday morning, and, unless a player needed special treatment, Monday was a day off. But when we began on our wonderful spell of success, the enthusiasm (perhaps it was just an excuse to spend a few more hours at Highbury) brought the players in on Mondays for light training and a chinwag, so that, eventually, Monday came to be regarded as a normal training day.

Monday would be devoted to a couple of loosening-up laps round the track, then a general rush to the head tennis court. Most of us became fanatics at this game, and, frequently, Tom would have to drive us off the court in order to get us home for lunch on time.

Tuesday was a slightly heavier day, starting with 8-12 laps round the track, skipping exercises, and kicking into goal with special soft shoes, invented by Herbert Chapman. They had a leather sole and a canvas top.

Most of us played golf in the afternoon, but, sometime, players came back for individual training, or a spell in the 'shooting box,' that ingenious arrangement where you could practise shooting at goal, and the ball would come back to you at awkward angles, speeding up your reactions and testing your ability to gather the ball from all angles.

Wednesday gave us not quite so much track-work, but more on the field. Goalkeepers were put through their paces, and, perhaps, players would try out skeleton plans, which might, or might not, be put into operation during the next match. Heading exercises came in for their share, and, of course, we frequently escaped for a game on the head-tennis court.

Much the same happened on a Thursday. Things slackened a bit the nearer we got to a match. But Friday was the big day. First thing Friday morning, we got our spikes on and Tom gave us sharp bursts, stops and starts (all footballers will know what I mean when I say this was most unpopular, yet probably one of the most beneficial exercises we had) and other track work. Then back to the gym for exercises, a spell on the punch ball, and a burst of skipping.

A bath, and we were ready for the real excitement of the day. Shortly before midday, the teams would go up on the notice board—First team, London Combination and Southern League sides. Then the first, with twelfth man, would accompany the manager and Tom Whittaker into the Board Room, while the reserves would go into the dressing-room with Joe Shaw, for the weekly team conferences on the morrow's game.

Our Board Room conferences, another Chapman institution, were very serious, but, at the same time, always interesting affairs. Sometimes, they went on so long that we got the cane from our wives for being home late for lunch. Every little detail of the last week's game, and the match on the following day, was discussed. On one occasion, I remember, we had gained a grand 4-1 victory away from home the previous week, but Chapman argued with us for one-and-a-half hours as that one goal shouldn't have been scored against the Arsenal!

These conferences moulded Arsenal. Chapman was a psychologist before the word became fashionable. Everything and everybody was discussed at these meetings… who was to take the place of the goalkeeper if he was injured, on which wing an injured player was to operate when a team was reshuffled, who took free kicks in certain parts of the field, penalty kick takers (you never saw any hesitation when Arsenal were awarded a penalty), and all the hundred and one situations which might arise in a big game, and, particularly, when a quick decision might mean the winning or losing of a vital cup-tie or league match.

The only time anybody ever gate-crashed the conference, was when the company making the 'Arsenal' film, came in to photograph us discussing a match. Needless to say, the talk was staged for the occasion!

Highbury, on match days, was a busy and exciting place. We players used to get there an hour to an hour-and-a-half before the game, and chat leisurely with friends or among ourselves until half-an-hour before the kick-off. Then Chapman appeared and 'threw' everybody out of the dressing-room, excepting the team and twelfth man, and Tom Whittaker. Even directors had to go. Then we would get the usual pep talk to ready us for the game.

CHAPTER 20

ALEXANDER THE GREAT

Nineteen-twenty-nine was a year of destiny for Arsenal— and myself. In that year the foundations were laid of the mighty side which was to sweep everything before it, and which was to become the greatest club side soccer history has known.

During the season which ended in April 1929, I had finally clinched my place in the Arsenal first team, while Herbert Roberts, Charlie Jones and Jack Lambert had also made their appearance. During the following summer, Herbert Chapman made two of his greatest 'buys,' to change, materially, the fortunes of our club.

He signed Alexander James and Clifford Sydney Bastin.

James was 28 and brought, from Preston, a reputation which cost Arsenal £9,000; Bastin was barely seventeen and had been a professional footballer a matter of weeks. What a contrast— and what a wing.

Brought together from clubs as far apart as Preston and Exeter; one a tough little Scot from Bellshill, hard as a nut, commercially-minded, determined to get much out of football, who had joined Arsenal because it offered the best possibilities of improving his position; the other, the son of sturdy West Country folk, who was born to be great, quiet, reserved, but, even then, with the infinite ability of being able to play football with the touch of the master... their destinies were irretrievably interwoven. The James-Bastin wing was a natural.

It was with more than ordinary interest that I met Alex when we reported from training that August. I had met Scots, many of them, in this great game of ours, but never one with an accent like Alex's. But when I got to understand his dialect, we had much to do with each other. Alex believes in speaking his mind, a failing, or virtue, of mine, so we had that in common.

Apart from his accent, Alex also had an amazing pair of legs "the most kicked legs in soccer," they were once called. However many times he was kicked during a match, and it was usually pretty often, the bruises never showed. And frequently, until he got used to it, Tom would say Alex was swinging the lead, when he went to the Whittaker 'surgery' for treatment.

I wrote very early on this book that whatever Arsenal did was news. The same might be said of Alex James. And I may say he gave the newspaper boys plenty to write about. Publicity followed him as naturally as children rally round the Pied Piper. He deliberately adopted the long-pants fashion, and retained the rather clinging garb, because it was expected of him. And, here, by the way, is the story of how he came to take up this exaggerated sartorial style.

Alex was playing at Stamford Bridge for Preston, against Chelsea, when Tom Webster did his usual brilliant cartoon in the *Daily Mail*. In it, Tom showed Alex wearing shorts which came down to his knees. Alex's shorts had been ordinary length up to then, but the idea so tickled him, he got a larger pair, and made himself look just like the cartoon!

One way, or another, Alex often seemed to be in trouble at Highbury. He had frequent brushes with the Old Boss, but, secretly, both were very fond of, and admired, each other. The first real battle he had with the club occurred at the end of 1930-31 season, when, for reasons of his own, he refused to re-sign for Arsenal. And this, of course, received great prominence in the sporting sheets.

The 'he has,' 'he hasn't,' 'he will,' 'he won't' controversy went on all through the summer, until Alex walked into Highbury and signed on the dotted line shortly before we were due to restart training for the new season. To celebrate, we rushed into the Arsenal band room, borrowed the instruments and played Alex on to the ground in state. I can still see Bill Patterson with the tuba wrapped round him, struggling through 'See the conquering Hero Comes,' one of the many tunes we were murdering!

Another of his ups and downs happened two seasons later, when Alex indicated that he didn't want to travel to Ireland on an Arsenal tour, immediately following the end of the season. Chapman took drastic disciplinary action, dropping Alex for the last match of the league programme. The little fellow retaliated by absenting himself from the Arsenal dinner the following week.

There was a spice of drama about that dinner. When we took our places at the tables in that very attractive room we used for such functions at the Café Royal, there were two vacant seats labelled, "A. James, Esq." and "Mrs. James." As strong-minded as ever, Alex had taken a step which, I know, must have been repugnant to him, of staying away from an official Arsenal function. The two seats remained vacant for some minutes after the first course was served, then Charlie Jones moved over to take the captain's place, and it was to him as "captain for this occasion" that the League Championship trophy was presented.

Alex was, and still is, the world's worst sailor (strange that his boy, also Alex, became a Merchant Navy sailor during the war), and wasn't too keen on being sent away on a sea trip in November of that year, when Herbert Chapman thought he needed a rest and a tone-up for the Cup ties soon to be with us. Alex always remembers that trip with distaste, for, crossing the Bay of Biscay, the ship ran into the worst storm for twenty years! He arrived at St. Katherine's Dock with a fair amount of luggage, including a dress suit, only to find that the ship on which he was to make his voyage, was a cargo vessel, carrying a load of sheep-skins to Bordeaux.

130

It is not generally known that Alex very nearly left Highbury for Derby County. I think that negotiations between the two clubs had reached the stage of naming the transfer fee, but when Alex was called in, he flatly refused to leave London, where, he said, he was very comfortable... and that was that.

There's no two ways about it, Alex was a great footballer, but, mind you, if Bob John hadn't been behind him when the wee fellow first arrived at Highbury, he wouldn't have been half as successful. At Preston he was a goal-scorer, with only hints here and there of the schemer he was to become. One season, he actually topped the Preston scorers. But when he took his place in the Arsenal forward line, he concentrated on making openings for others, and very rarely figured on our scoring sheet.

But one game, against Sheffield Wednesday, at Highbury, Alex startled the world by doing the hat-trick. He said, afterwards, that his eldest boy had told him he couldn't score goals if he tried, and that was Alex's answer. Another story I've heard Alex tell of that match is that "the goalkeeper threw two of them into the net for safety, and the third cannoned in off a full-back." Alex is a very funny man!

Breaking in on myself here, I must tell you a story of an incident at one of our Friday team conferences. After Mr. Allison had explained, at great length, a plan he had evolved with Alex playing the major role, he asked if there any questions. Alex, who had broodingly watched the demonstration on our famous football-pitch black board, calmly picked up ten of the figures representing Arsenal, leaving only 'himself' in the inside-left position. Rather surprised, Mr. Allison asked the reason for this action. Alex returned, "You won't need the others, they don't seem to be doing anything in this match!"

Which reminds me of the time when, with the blackboard not handy, we used eleven (full) lemonade bottles for the discussion, during which Mr. Allison was called away by an urgent phone message. On his return, he proceeded with the tactical talk. Suddenly, Ted Drake gravely remarked, "The centre-forward's drunk, Mr. Allison." And so he was, or rather had been... by Ted!

But to return to wee Alex. In July 1937, his long and brilliant career came to an end. During the summer he signed up with a pools firm as a director at £40 a week, and so his twinkling feet were lost to soccer as a performer.

Alex, refused permission by the Football Association to come back into the game as a manager, and also not allowed to play for Northampton in wartime football, nevertheless, did not go entirely out of the game. In the summer of 1939 he took a coaching job in Poland, and came back to this country only a few weeks before war was declared. He once moaned that he couldn't understand the way the Poles talked. Perhaps it was the other way round! Alex also played a couple of games for Drumcondra in the League of Ireland Shield early in the first season of the war. A humorous memory for him was, after the first match, against St. James Gate, the Drumcondra management wanted to pay him his fee in threepenny pieces and sixpences taken at the gate that afternoon.

Alex's other love, probably more deeply-rooted than football, is golf. If he had not become a top-line footballer, I think he would have been a golf professional. Even with his other interests, he got down to single figures, and once won the Harry Vardon trophy at South Herts, his home club. But the best round he ever played, he told me, was at Balwearie (Kircaldy), where, to settle a bet, he played a round using only one club, a No. 4 iron. He equalled the scratch score of 74.

Alex, like myself, abhorred dirty play, and, although he frequently got the thin edge of the wedge on the field, he never once retaliated. So it was surprising when, one day, he told me he probably held a record unique in soccer....he is probably the only man who was ever sent off the field two weeks running. It happened when he was playing for Raith Rovers in his early days. In the first game, he got involved in a scrimmage, and, when the dust cleared, found that he had been ordered off the field. It was no consolation to him to learn that later in the match a linesman drew the referee's attention to the fact he had sent the wrong man off and that the referee "squared" the mistake by sending the real offender to the pavilion to join Alex. The following week, in the return match against the same team, and with the same referee, Alex again got his marching orders for a trivial offence.

The sequel was amusing. When Alex came up before the Disciplinary Committee for "judgment," the chairman delivered him a strong lecture, ending with the words, "Now, young fellow, don't let me see you here again. Case dismissed. Next offender please." The next offender was....Alex, up on the second charge. This time he got a month's suspension!

Alex played in two Cup-winning Arsenal teams, but has no medal to show for either match. His generosity is responsible for that. He gave them both away.

A few days after we beat Huddersfield in 1930, Alex sent his winner's medal to his friend, Mr. Robert Morrison, a former director of Raith Rovers, Alex's first big club. In a letter accompanying the gift, Alex wrote: "No one deserves it more than you, for I can honestly say that there would never have been any Alex James but for old Bob." The latter reference was to the help Mr. Morrison gave him when he was a struggling young player in Scotland.

Six years later, Alex gave way the medal he won when we beat Sheffield United, this time to Pat Beasley, who lost his place in the Wembley team when Ted Drake was passed fit at the eleventh hour. Pat refused it at first, saying he would wait until the decision of the F.A. was made known, following Arsenal's application to have another specially struck for

Beasley. The application was refused, so Alex handed his medal over.

As a matter of historical interest, Alex played his last game for Arsenal v Rotterdam at the Feyenoord Stadium during our Dutch tour two seasons before the war.

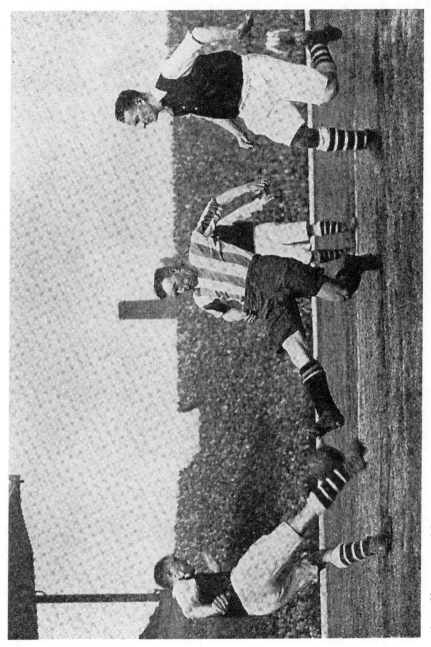

A split-second interception, and Davies (West Bromwich) is beaten for the ball. Right is Herbert Roberts.

The Lost Captain.

(Herbert Chapman, January 6th, 1934).

THE last whistle has sounded, the great game is over,
  O was ever a field left so silent as this;
The scene a bright hour since, how empty it is!
What desolate splendour the shadows now cover.
The captain has gone. The splendour was his.

He made no farewell, no sign has he given
  That for him nevermore shall the big ball roll,
Nor the players he urged on, from his strong heart and soul,
Strive again with his skill, as they always have striven,
Not again will he hear when the crowd shouts "Goal!"

But somewhere . . . somewhere his spirit will quicken
  With victors and vanquished. For now he has cast
In his lot with the Olympians of old who outlast
This human encounter, this football so stricken
That it seemed for a moment to die when he passed.

Who shall challenge his name, who shall challenge the laurel
  We hold out to him through the twilight? His love
Was in beauty of action, and clean limbs that move
With the pride of high combat above the mean quarrel.
He led others to share it, And that is enough.

Not yet for those others the Full-Time is blowing.
  The ball will roll on, they will cheer with their throats aflame;
They will think how this steel-minded man in his fame
Had dreamed while he worked, a dream ever glowing,
Of the glory of Greece in an English game.

T.M.

Tribute
to the memory of the late
Mr. Herbert Chapman.

Joe Shaw's tribute to the "Old Boss."

136

Off duty in Germany. Stanley Matthews and the author pause between shots.

The *"Prince of the Potteries"* in action.

Prize-giving after a petola match in Paris.

Not what it seems. The camera catches the author and
Buchanan (Chelsea) in an unusual pose.

Captain of England for the first time. England v Italy at Highbury, 1934. The author introduces the late Prince Arthur of Connaught to George Male. Behind is Signor Grandi, then Italian Ambassador.

The F.A. party watch Stanley Cullis (nearest camera) and England's captain lay a wreath on the Tomb of the Unknown Soldier, Bucharest, May, 1939.

CHAPTER 21

ARSENAL AND OLD FACES

Looking back down Memory Lane at my stay at Highbury, always makes for nostalgic thoughts. Happy ones, though. We had some grand players, and, although it is always said 'put an Arsenal jersey on a player and he'll get into his international team,' I think all the men from Highbury who received caps deserved them.

And we had a few while I was there. In fact, at one time or the other, we could have turned out a national team ourselves. What about this side for England?—Moss; Male; Hapgood; Crayston; Roberts; Copping; Hulme; Jack; Drake; Bastin and Denis Compton. Then there's Les Compton, Ray Bowden, Alf Baker, George Marks, Jack Butler, Laurie Scott, Bernard Joy and Alf Kirchen.

And don't forget Alex James, W. Harper and young Gordon Bremner for Scotland, Horace Cumner, Bob John, Bryn Jones, Charlie Jones, Les Jones and Dan Lewis for Wales and Kennedy and Mackie for Ireland, among others.

Yes, Highbury was a good breeding-place for internationals. Some, of course, were capped before they arrived with us, but most were trained so well, that the International Selectors couldn't afford to miss them! As Jack Barker, the Derby County centre-half said to Eric Brook before the match with Italy at Highbury, "You've got to take off your hats to these Arsenal players. If one of us were to drop out, another Arsenal man would step in!" We had seven Arsenal players in that match— Bastin, Bowden, Copping, Drake, Male, Moss and myself.

Or Wolverhampton on February 5, 1936, when six Arsenal players were in the England side against Wales....Male, Crayston, Bowden, Drake, Bastin, and myself.

That game, incidentally, will always remain one of the sharpest memories in Ted Drake's career.

In the first fifteen minutes he sustained a nasty-looking cut over one eye, went off and came back after treatment. Then he was badly shaken after suffering one of the heaviest falls I have seen on a football field. And, finally, he was injured on the left knee, following a heavy tackle by Hanford. This completed Ted's day out. Later that evening he was taken to hospital, and, after being examined under an anaesthetic, was operated on for cartilege trouble. He also had concussion, and was out for weeks — coming back shortly before the Final to win the Cup against Sheffield United with the only goal of the match.

Ted is a great-hearted player, who, in his career, suffered many hard knocks, but still came up smiling. His ready wit enlivened countless train journeys and after-match discussions, often when we needed a little encouragement. He has often told me cricket is his favourite game, and well can I believe that. Ted is ready at any hour of the day or night to discuss cricket and cricketers. And he has a fund of stories, which, although we heard them several times, always came up fresh.

One of his humorous memories he used to tell against himself. As you probably know, Ted was a county player (for Hampshire) and recalls that his first championship game was against Notts. Ted, batting No. 9, came in to face the last three balls of a Larwood over, surely one of the most testing starts any young batsman has made.

Ted, as he says, played a perfectly straight bat to the first ball, but it whistled past into the keeper's hands. A similar shot to the next delivery, and the ball, catching the edge of his bat, scudded away down to third man. Ted went tearing up the pitch, but the batsman at the other end (also a colt), said 'No,' and sent him back to face the last ball of

Larwood's over. Ted scored off this, and the other batsman was glad to run....Voce was bowling at the other end!

Ted took guard, and while surveying the field, casually asked wicket-keeper Ben Lilley how Voce was bowling... "too good for you," was the grim reply... and it was. Over went Ted's castle and our hero retired with this record of his début... Drake, b. Voce 1.

Joe Hulme touched the heights when he was wearing an Arsenal shirt. And he ably played his part in the Arsenal plan with that terrific burst of speed down the right touch-line. He was like a greyhound waiting in the trap for the hare, when Alex had the ball in No-Man's-Land outside our penalty area. A long punt out to the right, cleverly beating the defence, and Joe was away down the line with that raking stride which used to break full-backs' hearts. No Stanley Matthews shuffle for our Joe.

Alex, of course, was the feed for Cliff Bastin on the left-wing. A different type of player from Hulme was Cliff. Quiet and unemotional, living almost in a world of his own by reason of his defective hearing, Bastin is probably the coolest player I ever saw. Nothing ruffles or upsets him.

An instance of this came early in his career — in the semi-final against Hull City at Leeds in 1930. We were two down with only twenty minutes to go, and, virtually, out of the Cup. Hull had scored twice while we were struggling to unravel Bill McCracken's offside trap, and finding it heavy going. Every time Lambert or Hulme went after the ball, they were greeted by the maddening blast of the referee's whistle, calling them offside.

There was a touch of luck about both Hull goals, but, on the run of the play, they deserved them. In the sixteenth minute a Dan Lewis clearance dropped in front of Howieson, Hull's international inside-left, who promptly returned it high into the goalmouth. Lewis had the lob well recovered, but, somehow, the ball slipped in between his arms and the cross-bar. The second goal I turned into the Arsenal goal while trying to clear Duncan's shot.

That's how it was with three-quarters of the game gone. The Hull supporters were sounding our death knell with rattles and firing toy pistols, which made a tremendous din. Then Davie Jack got a great goal, such as only he could score, but it still didn't seem possible we could equalise, until Cliff strolled through the packed defence and scored a wizard goal. We nearly mobbed him, and even the Hull supporters cheered. But he took it all without turning a hair.

Another invaluable goal he got for Arsenal put us into the 1932 Final. The semi-final against Manchester City had only two minutes to run, we were all very tired and dreading the match going into extra time. Cliff got the ball in midfield, and set off on his way toward the City goal. Some forty yards out he transferred to Jack Lambert who dashed on, keeping control of the ball, although forced out toward the wing. A few yards from the goal-line he crossed, and Cliff, positioning himself perfectly, glided the ball past Langford to win the match.

An amazing personality, this boy, who at the age of eleven, was scoring goals in an Exeter Schools' League, with a young sports master named Stanley Rous from a nearby Teachers' College, in charge; who turned pro on his seventeenth birthday; who had won every honour possible in top-class soccer before he was 21. The secret of his success? I don't know, but I do know why he and Alex James were such a great partnership. Alex used to say, "You stay out on the line, Cliff, and I'll give you the ball." And Cliff was always where Alex knew to find him. Look at the 1930 Final, when Alex took that quick free-kick. A short pass to Bastin, waiting in position, a return pass… and we were one up.

I always remember one story of Cliff. In 1933 we were chosen to tour with England in Italy, my first cap, and Cliff's second. Naturally, Bastin was a household name — the previous season he had set up a League record by scoring 33 goals from the wing — and he was very popular with the Italians. So much so, that he was followed about everywhere. One day he and I left the hotel for a walk, closely followed by a bunch of Italians who would keep asking how many 'goala' Cliff was going to score on the morrow. Exasperated, I told Cliff to tell them 'eight.' He did so, and we continued on our way unmolested.

Next morning, to my horror, I saw that several of the Italian papers carried the banner headline, "Il Bastino will score eight goals today." The men we thought were fans were, in fact, newspapermen. Anyway, Cliff got the goal by which we drew, and one of the newspapermen gallantly covered up his forecast by saying that goal was so good, it was worth eight!

Cliff and I were also involved in another sort of test. We were both on holiday at Butlin's Camp at Clacton when we were asked to assist boxing champion Len Harvey to judge a parade of bathing belles. Armed with measuring tapes, we set about our task with enthusiasm, and, although some of the girls hadn't much glamour, I think we came to a perfectly amicable settlement of the prize!

Davie Jack was a type on his own in soccer. Tall, impeccably dressed, he looked more like a bank manager or successful business man than a professional footballer. If I ever had to make a set decision on the best player I ever saw, I would plump for David. As far as I was concerned, Jack was as good as his master— and better.

When he came to Highbury from Bolton, David had his own ideas about training. After a couple of appearances at Highbury he failed to turn up for training, and Tom, rather worried about his new 'chick' went out to where David was lodging. Mrs. Jack opened the door and said David was in the back room resting. He was, with his feet on the mantelpiece, and smoking like a furnace.

147

To Tom's enquiry as to his health, David replied, "Oh! I'm all right, but I always had Thursdays off at Bolton!" But that misunderstanding was cleared up and genial Tom Whittaker soon got him into line with the Arsenal scheme. Not that David was a rebel, or swollen-headed, or anything like. He was, and is, a splendid chap.

David was practically a chain-smoker — and he also liked chocolates. Which reminds me of the time when we were on a Brighton training trip. I was awakened one morning about 1 a.m. by a hacking cough, and on investigation, found David busily typing his weekly article for the London *Evening Standard* — alternately puffing at a cigarette and taking bites from succulent looking chocolates!

The ex-Bolton star, who is down in the record books as the scorer of the first-ever goal at Wembley, and whose goal also beat Manchester City in 1926, had a swerve that looked so simple, yet was ghost-like. This combined with the ability of effortlessly changing feet in front of goal, or of seeming to hit the ball off the 'wrong' foot, made Davie a very dangerous customer to tackle.

Davie always had a business mind — it is said he kept a daily record of the number of times he could head a tennis ball — and when he hung up his boots, he stayed in football to become Southend's manager. When Southend (the club, not the town) moved into Chelmsford, Davie went back to work in his old profession, banking. Incidentally, he turned out several times for Barclay's Bank in wartime football, and, in one game, against United Hospitals, played the first half at right-back, and switched to his favourite position of inside-right after the interval. He scored five in a row... a sure sign the old Jack talent was there. After a spell as manager of a thriving greyhound racing track at Sunderland, Davie signed as Middlesbrough manager a few months back.

And so to Bryn Jones. I've nothing personal against Bryn, but I'll always have it that Arsenal should never have paid £14,000 to Wolves for his transfer. It was unfair to Jones, and to the rest of the team. The little Welshman, an ex-pit boy from Merthyr Tydfil, came to us like a man with a millstone round his neck. He was a grand footballer, but I am convinced the responsibility of being the most expensive player of all time was too much for Bryn and he never played like a £14,000 player for Arsenal. He is a quiet little fellow with crinkly black hair, and has a ready shot in either foot, but a different type of player from wee Alex. We had to change our whole style of play when Bryn stepped in to fill the gap left by Alex retiring.

Another Welshman, my great pal Bob John was the finest half-back I ever played behind. Pity we had to split up when England played Wales. Bob had one superstition nobody could shake, and which made him very unhappy when he was asked to captain the Arsenal, or his national side. He always liked to be last on the field, a superstition shared by other famous players, among them Vic Woodley, I believe.

Bob was a great player anywhere, and a fine team man. Remember when we played Newcastle in the 1932 Final? Alex James' breakdown meant a reshuffling of the team. George Male went left-half — his first cup-tie, this was — and Bob outside-left, with Cliff as his partner. And Bob got our goal, the all-important first-score at Wembley, which however, failed to win the day for us. As the world knows, Allen scored his famous 'disputed' goal to equalise, and, later, got another to clinch the match for Newcastle.

Charlie Buchan was one of the brainiest players the game has produced. His, actually, was the first suggestion that started the Arsenal using the defensive-offensive plan always associated with Herbert Chapman. Here's how it happened.

At the beginning of the 1925-26 season, Arsenal struck a bad patch and lost all but two of their first seven games, the last by 7-0 at Newcastle. On the following Monday there was another game due, this time against West Ham at Upton Park.

At the team conference on the morning before this game, Charlie raised the point that Arsenal couldn't go on in this fashion, and that a change of tactics must be introduced. Chapman asked him for suggestions, and Charlie expressed the desire for a defensive centre-half or 'third full-back,' as he became known.

Chapman agreed this was a possibility, but his quick-thinking brain saw that the scheme was lacking something, and that by turning an attacking centre-half into a defender, some of the attacking power was being lost. So Charlie suggested a roving inside-forward. Chapman quickly visualised the possibilities of this plan, and after a long discussion as to ways and means, it was put into operation that very afternoon, with Andy Neil (also known with Brighton and Kilmarnock) as the roving inside-left. Butler was the centre-half. Arsenal won, four nothing!

The scheme got better and better as the season wore on. Later, Jimmy Ramsay took over the job, and then, when he was hurt, Billy Blyth stepped in to form that great wing with Hoar. Arsenal finished second in the league that year, and were beaten in the sixth round of the Cup at Swansea, the only time the Welsh club reached the semi-final, by the way. The following year (my first season), we got to the Final, losing by the only goal to Cardiff.

That, then, was the birth of the Arsenal plan, so ably carried to perfection by Herbie Roberts, Bob John and Alex James.

Buchan, a man of great strength, a last war Guardsman, and a C.S.M. in a London Home Guard company during this war, who, on retirement, became an astute football critic with the *News-Chronicle*, figured in one of the most interesting football transfers of all time. The transfer fee fixed when he left Sunderland for Highbury was £2,000, with a proviso that Sunderland were paid £100 for every goal scored by Buchan for Arsenal in his first season. Charlie got nineteen in the

League and three in the Cup, so his final transfer fee was £4,200.

And so all my old comrades pass before me in mental review. Jack Lambert, an ordinary type of centre-forward, who touched the heights when brushed with the magic of Arsenal. Lambert, in his early days, when trying to make himself into a great centre-forward, fell foul of a certain section of Highbury supporters, who, every time he came on to the field, made it plain that, whatever else the team did, anything he was involved in was all wrong with them. Chapman was so incensed by this that he took the unusual step of publicly defending his player in a newspaper article. Lambert later settled down and, of course, played for Arsenal in two Cup Finals. Poor old Jack — 'Honest' Jack, Chapman called him. He did a great job of work for Arsenal when he took over our nursery at Margate, but lost his life in a road accident a few months after the start of the war.

Frank Moss, one of the best goalkeepers I ever saw, but a man who carried a hoodoo on his shoulder, or rather in it. A great goalkeeper, with all the pluck in the world; Billy Blyth, as good a golfer as footballer; Tom Parker, my colleague in many dour struggles, a very fine back and one of the most consistent players I have ever come across, absolutely dependable in every game, the man who saved my son's life; Alf Baker, Herbert Roberts, one of the most gentlemanly soccer pros I ever met. Herbie and I were contemporaries in the closest sense. I gained my place in the Arsenal first team shortly before Roberts, a slim, rangy lad from Oswestry, a right-half, bred and born, who was destined to be the most talked-of centre-half big football has known. Not until Herbie took over from Jack Butler at centre-half did the 'Chapman third-back game' really get under way. Herbie was a natural for Chapman's scheme....and always stoutly upheld that the scheme saved soccer, not spoiled it.

We all liked and admired this quietly spoken, deep thinking red-head, and I know all connected with Arsenal of those halcyon days felt as grieved as I when we heard of his sudden death in June 1944. Herbie, who never kicked a football after being hurt against Middlesbrough, at Highbury nearly seven years before, succumbed in the Middlesex Hospital to erysipelas.

He was one of the safest players I ever saw, so that, perhaps, my outstanding memory of Herbie was the match in which he put two goals into the Arsenal net in two minutes, a rare occurrence at the best of times, and, where he was concerned, very nearly impossible. It was against Derby County at Highbury on October 8, 1932, and we were leading comfortably 3-1 late in the second half. Then Dally Duncan crossed a twirling in-swinger. Roberts lunged at the greasy ball, and it ricocheted into the net. Two minutes later, exactly the same thing happened. Poor Herbie's face was a mixture of bewilderment and chagrin. But, as Herbert Chapman put it, he saw the humorous side later.

There was a sequel to this match. Some time later, a large square envelope arrived at Highbury, addressed to Herbie. It contained the original of a cartoon, drawn by Ripley, and included in his "Believe it or Not" series, of Roberts' freak performance.

But I remember another goal scored by Roberts some seven months earlier, which put us into the semi-final. We were playing Huddersfield, at Huddersfield, in the sixth round of the Cup, and there was something in the nature of genius which prompted that goal, and victory. We forced a corner in the first two minutes while the crowd were milling about on the touch-line, so great was the excitement and so high the hopes of Huddersfield folk of seeing mighty Arsenal get a cup knock-out. As Joe Hulme (years later to be transferred to the Town, and to finish his career in a Wembley Cup Final with the club) was fighting his way through the crowd — police had to clear a passage for his run — to take the corner, Herbie was strolling leisurely upfield. Twelve players, six of us and half-a-dozen of the other, were gathered in the Huddersfield penalty area, when Hulme took the kick, a high curving ball, driven into the glare of the blazing sun. By this time, Herbie had casually crossed the penalty line, and, before the Huddersfield defenders realised the danger, had headed the ball into the net. There was something typically, supremely confident and cheeky about that goal. Then he came back to help the Arsenal defence in his 'rightful' job of keeping out the opposing forwards. We won by that goal, beat Manchester City by Cliff Bastin's last minute goal in the semi-final, but lost to Newcastle at Wembley.

As an epilogue to poor Herbie, perhaps I could quote the remark of Alf Young, who, after being congratulated on his fine play in an International Trial match, thanked the well-wisher, and, in the same breath, said, "All the same Herbie Roberts is the 'Daddy' of them all."

Then there is blue-chinned Wilf Copping, whose motto was "First man into a tackle never gets hurt," but who was never cautioned or sent off — and who never shaved before a match — Jack Crayston, quietly-spoken, quick thinking half-back, who fitted so well into the Arsenal scheme, and who would sooner cut off his leg than go over the ball at a man; Denis Compton, brilliantly erratic with a spark of genius somewhere in his football make-up, but who lived, talked and ate cricket. Perhaps Denis will turn out the finest batsman of all time. I hope so, he's got it in him. As L. V. Manning so aptly put it once, "Denis works at football, but plays at cricket."

Of Horace Cope, the man whose place I took in the Arsenal side so many years ago, I would like to give one story which illustrates his sterling character. On the Friday when the team list, carrying my name for the first time, was posted on the board, I felt elated — and miserable as well. Horace was a club mate, and a player I greatly respected for his clever and thoughtful play, and I knew that it must have been a bit of a blow for him to be supplanted by a youngster, not long on the club's books.

Later that morning he followed me into the bathroom at Highbury, where I was washing my hands, and, after a few moments silence, said, "Well, lad, this is your chance, take it, and the best of luck to you." A moment, and a sportsman, to remember.

Before I close this chapter on my colleagues, I must tell this story of young Charlie Walsh, who played only one first team game for the 'Reds'....that ill-fated match against Walsall the world won't let us forget. He had long been hounding Herbert Chapman for a chance in the first team, and, at last, our manager gave it him. He rested Lambert, and included Walsh in the cup team.

Walsh was a self-confident youngster, very keen to show his paces, and, a few minutes before the game, was sitting quite composedly in the dressing-room at Walsall when Herbert walked in for his last minute pep talk. He said to Walsh, "Now, son, I'm expecting a lot of things from you this afternoon. I'm relying on you to show me your best, etc., etc.," Walsh listened and replied, "O.K., Mr. Chapman, I'm ready to play the game of my life." Herbert said, "Good lad, you'll do," and then, just as he was turning away, remarked, "Oh, by the way, you'd better put your stockings on or the crowd will laugh at you."

Walsh, inwardly a nervous wreck, had put his football boots on, but was still wearing his socks and suspenders.

CHAPTER 22

PRINCE OF THE POTTERIES

I was once asked a leading question by a sharply inquisitive friend as to what was the greatest game I ever saw Stanley Matthews play. He had a sardonic sense of humour. I could not, in fairness to myself, and to Stan, admit he played his best-ever game against me! My answer was that I couldn't separate his performances (a) v Ireland at Old Trafford, November 16, 1938, when his wing partner Billy Hall scored five times in a row; (b) v Czecho-Slovakia at Tottenham, 1937; (c) his grand exhibition when we laid the Hampden bogey in April 1939; or (d) his dogged brilliance in that incident-laden match against Italy at Milan the following month.

The Czech match, in which I didn't play, but watched from the stand, was, perhaps, the one he'll remember longest. We had one of the toughest fights in recent years before we beat the men from Skoda-land, and only the wizardry of Matthews made it possible that day. It was thrust and parry all the way, with science at a premium, and the scores were level at 4-4 when the crowd starting wending their way homewards in the gathering darkness a few minutes before the end.

Stan had already scored twice, and, even his electric heels were a little slowed by the heavy going, when he picked up yet another loose ball in midfield, and, sliding his way through, rammed it past Planicka, the Czech goalkeeper—and a good one at that—for the winning goal. And it was Stan's third that afternoon with his left foot!

Stan really is one of the greatest wingers I've ever seen or played against, and I always enjoyed our clashes. He made me work harder in those matches than any other winger I met. But I don't think Stanley got very much change out of Arsenal, whenever our league engagements pitted us with Stoke City.

Arsenal always played as a team, and, knowing full well that my colleagues were taking care of the rest of the Stoke side, I was able to go all out on the task of stopping the Prince of the Potteries.

Early on in my career I realised that the only way to play Stanley properly was to make sure *he never got the ball*. He likes the slow rolling pass, and is at his most dangerous when standing still. So if the pass to him is blocked, Matthew's effectiveness is cut down to nil. If Stanley gets the ball, it is fatal to hesitate in your tackle. He is surprisingly fast when he is past you, and takes a lot of catching.

But Matthews really offered only a simple problem, because he treats the matter of beating a full-back as a challenge to his own skill, and he would sooner beat a man than get rid of the ball straight away. Whereas it is the less experienced winger who sets the harder problem, for he often cracks the ball straight back in the middle, or passes to a colleague before you've time to get in and tackle him. That makes you think, and also run about.

The man who did give me the most trouble, for about half-an-hour, was young Billy Warnes, son of old Rube Warnes, who was playing outside-right against me in an Arsenal trial match. And this is the first time I've told anybody this story. Billy was getting the ball correctly from the men behind, and hitting it away first time to his inside men while I was still three of four yards from him. His centring and passing were deadly accurate and every first-time effort came off that day. In the end I overcame the danger by standing on top of him. But that's the sort of danger man a winger can be.

I always played what I call an 'angle' game. I coined that phrase myself, and it is actually only close positional play. It was effective for wingers who stood wide out on the wings and dilly-dallied long enough to attempt to draw me out of position before centring. But often I wouldn't be drawn, which frequently annoyed people, who said, "Hapgood is being stand-offish!"

The benefit of the angle game was that I smothered a winger, and left him so little space to cross the ball that, frequently, I would block his centre with my head or chest. Otherwise he would get his centre in over my left shoulder, where it would either go behind or straight into the goalkeeper's hands, or, the other way, over my right shoulder, and be of little use to his forwards. Of course, I'm talking theoretically. It didn't always work out, but it certainly helped during my long career.

By the way, it may surprise many people to know that I played against one of the greatest wings of all time—Jackson and Kelly of Huddersfield—when I was barely eighteen. I still have the newspaper cutting which states... "In the first ten minutes Jackson looked like winning the game on his own, but then this young defender (Hapgood) took charge."

But there's one winger I've got no answer to—the 'dirty' player. Thank heavens they were few and far between. I met only two really dirty players during my whole career. But, even then, while I was massaging my bruises, I consoled myself with the fact that they couldn't beat me fairly, so had to resort to other methods.

CHAPTER 23

BEST-EVER TEAM

Having had a fair chance to assess the merits of the leading players of the last three decades, men who have made their mark in the golden era of soccer, I am one who firmly believes the modern footballer is as good, if not better, than his ancient counterpart of the cloth-cap era.

I've played with, or against, the best for seventeen years, sufficient time to assess their merits and demerits. And, greatly daring, I'll attempt to name the team I would like to have played in, if it were possible to muster them in the same club jerseys.

To my mind, the majority of the positions are instantaneously filled. The only place I find it hard to discriminate is at centre-forward, so I've taken the easy way out of naming three men, leaving the reader to fill in his favourite choice from the short list.

My goalkeeper is Harry Hibbs, rated by some schools as the best of all time, by others as second only to Sam Hardy. Never having had the full opportunity of playing with Hardy, I cannot make any statement as to his capabilities, so Hibbs will do for me. A fine type of man, who never let his country, club, colleagues or himself down.

I had the best possible chance of studying, in particular, the play of the great full-backs… Roy Goodall (who captained the first England side I played in), Ernie Blenkinsop, Tom Cooper, Sam Wadsworth, Ernie Catlin (who displaced me in the England side for nearly a full season), Tom Parker (my first Arsenal colleague), Bert Sproston, Warney Cresswell, George Male, and the rest. My choice for partner is Male, with whom I worked up a grand combination for Arsenal and England.

George came to Highbury from an amateur club as a wing-half-back, and it was at left-half that he gained his first Cup medal. But he was a better full-back than half, though, frequently, he reverted to the middle line for Arsenal wartime games. Male, incidentally, was the only man to whom I ever relinquished the England captaincy after I had once been given the honour. My first game as England captain was against Italy at Highbury on November 14, 1934, and I held the position, with one break, for thirty-seven games, my last being against Wales at Wembley on January 27, 1943.

The only exception was at Helsingfors, against Finland, on May 20, 1937, when I came back to the side after being kept out by Catlin for six games. Male had been appointed captain for the tour, and retained that honour when I regained my position in the side.

However, to get on. My choice for right-half, unanimously proposed and seconded by myself, is Willis Edwards, of Leeds United, who, although I never had the opportunity of studying him in front of me in an international side, I saw frequently in club matches. An ideal half-back, who could go forward or back at any time, and all the time.

For centre-half I choose the player to whom I handed over the England captaincy at the end of my long run... Stanley Cullis, of Wolverhampton Wanderers. An intelligent, defensive centre-half, who varied his play by attacking when the situation warranted this method. Stanley has mannerisms which sometimes annoy onlookers, but nothing ruffles him. He goes his own way, thoughtfully, always looking for the opportunity of a crack down the middle.

Apropos of nothing, I must tell you a story of Stan. He is always studying, arguing, or theorising, and is one of the many lads who is making soccer a stepping stone to a good job when he retires. On this particular tour somebody had been chipping Cullis about his study of foreign languages and, particularly, about French, which was Stan's particular interest at the moment. Stan took it all like the good-natured fellow he is, and bided his time.

We were out sight-seeing one morning and the chipper in-chief (I forget his name but he took the sequel in good part) told Stan to ask a benevolent looking Frenchman the direction to a certain place of interest. Some of the doubters, naturally, expected Stan to take out a French-English dictionary and haltingly stumble his way through a couple of simple sentences. But with an admiring audience, and without turning a hair, he launched into fluent French in the manner born!

At left-half I look no further than Bob John, my Arsenal colleague for so many years. I have previously mentioned Bob, so will pass on with the comforting thought that I never wanted to play behind a better player.

The forwards, forgive me, with one exception, wear an Arsenal shirt. Here they are….Hulme, Jack, James and Bastin. Try as I can, there's no way I can fault this quartette.

But the centre-forward position is tricky. Here's my three nominees I cannot separate. Different in their own way, but great players all….Dixie Dean, a wizard with his feet, but just as deadly with his head, as strong as a house, and just as hard to knock off the ball, as clean in his play as a new pin, a great sportsman, and a trier to the end. Dixie was always a tough handful, not only because he used to roam out on to the wings, taking the centre-half with him, and, frequently, slipping him, making it extremely hard for the rest of the defence to keep some sort of order.

Hughie Gallagher, greatest centre-forward ever to come over the Border, who hunched himself over the ball in a way that made it almost impossible to dispossess him unless he was to be knocked over, a bobby-dazzler dribbler with a flashing shot delicately angled to beat even the most agile goalkeeper, his only drawback a fiery temper, which far too many players took advantage of—I always thought he was more shinned against than shinning—the centre-forward of

160

whom Herbie Roberts once told me, "Hughie is perhaps the most elusive antagonist who bluffed me into going the wrong way." His smallness and lightness of foot made him difficult to 'get at.' Always trying new tricks was the little fellow who learned his football in the streets of Bellshill with Alex James….and the third, George Camsell, rather like Dixie Dean, perhaps not quite as good with his head, but a deadly shot from anywhere near the penalty area, and terrifically fast.

Well, there you are, that's my choice. Have another look at them and then argue. I have included myself because I would have been honoured to play in this team:

Hibbs (Birmingham); Male (Arsenal); Hapgood (Arsenal); Edwards (Leeds Utd); Cullis (Wolves); John (Arsenal); Hulme (Arsenal); Jack (Arsenal); Dean (Everton) or Gallacher (Chelsea and Newcastle) or Camsell (Middlesbrough); James (Arsenal); and Bastin (Arsenal).

CHAPTER 24

FAN MAIL AND PRESS GANG

In the early part of 1943, within a few weeks of each other, I received two communications. With the only comment that I shall treasure them to the end of my days, I give them fully.

The first, a postcard, came from M-Stammlager XXB, Germany, and read: *"Dear Eddie, I have been asked by the boys of this working party to congratulate you, and we all hope by the time this arrives in England that you have created a record.* (It arrived a few days after I played in my 43rd international). *So here's wishing you the best of luck. Sincerely, Albert Jennings, 37133, W.P. 272."*

That tribute from a prisoner of war, who, in the midst of his troubles, could spare a thought for one who was free to play football in the Old Country, left me a little breathless when it arrived. I hope to meet Albert Jennings when he returns home.

The other letter, very much longer, was forwarded to me by the Soviet Relations Branch, Ministry of Information, and was from Alexander Divochkin, captain of the Central Red Army House team….and Hero of the Soviet Union. Read it, as I did, with pride:

"Dear Mr. Hapgood, I have read with greatest interest Mr. Jimmy Bolton's article, published in our paper "Red Sports", about your football team. It was most pleasant to learn of the high opinion you hold of Soviet football and that you are looking forward to future meetings of Soviet and English footballers. I, too, fervently hope these will take place.

I am your colleague in football. In peacetime I always struggle for honours of Central Red Army House team on football field. Also, I often indulged in ski-ing and more than once participated in All Union sprinting competitions.

I am an artilleryman and was one of the first to come to grips with the Fascists. On the night of June 22, 1941 I was frontier guard on duty at state border. My fighting friends and I were the first to receive perfidious blows dealt by enemy. We defended our outpost against German rascals in an unequal battle lasting twelve hours. Hence I have been on the battlefield ever since that first day of war.

Once my battery happened to be encircled by the enemy. For two days we were without food, but since there was not any shortage of ammunition, we continued to fight in a sea of fire under a shower of enemy shells. Quite unexpectedly, one fell among a pile of ammunition. I dashed into the blaze, my greatcoat catching alight, my jacket beginning to flare up. I was dominated by one thought—our ammunition, if blown up, would be the end of us all. Helped by Gun Commander Sumny and Marksmen Suslov and Sisoev, I managed to drag boxes away from the fire, thus enabling our battery to keep fighting successfully. But the very moment the fire was extinguished, the enemy started another attack.

I rushed to the gun and opened a tornado of fire. Suddenly, the gun carriage of my cannon was shot through. I dashed to another cannon, but a little later its barrel was damaged. What to do next? Nearby, I noticed a third cannon with a wounded Red Army man lying alongside. Crawling quickly, I rescued the gun and opened fire. I continued firing until reinforcements arrived and the enemy encirclement was broken. However, what I did, anyone else could have done equally well. (No wonder they gave him a hero's medal— E.H.)

Here at the front I am often grateful to Soviet sports for making me courageous, hardy and strong. Many football colleagues of mine are at the front, too, keeping fighting score and wiping out the Germans.

163

You certainly have heard of the Leningrad football team 'Dynamo,' which went bravely through all difficulties of blockade, yet nevertheless managed to train reserves for the front. Footballers Mikhailov, Federov, Oreshkin, and others have trained hundreds of skilled skiers, grenade gunners and swimmers. Last summer the footballers of Leningrad undertook a trip throughout the country and organised a number of inter-town sporting events. In Omsk, Leningrad footballers won three matches against a team called 'Progress,' Omsk scratch team and N. School. I am sure that you, skilled master of football, must be interested in football matches played in Moscow this year. Team 'Spartak' went to the top during the autumn football season in the capital. Spartak displayed high class technique without suffering a single defeat or draw.

I heartily shake your hand. Give my compliments to your club friends and tell them that our sportsmen are fighting in the front lines with redoubled energy, and in each of us burns the desire to wipe the Fascist rascals from the face of the earth."

If as I hope, my ambition to visit Moscow is realised after the war, I hope to shake your hand personally, Comrade Divochkin, and those of your gallant comrades.

Those two are, perhaps, the best-remembered from my post-bag over the years. Another I treasure highly, also received during the war, but from an old friend, not a stranger across the sea, was sent me by Andy Beattie, Preston North End and Scotland full-back, who later went out to the Middle East. I hope Andy won't mind if I quote it:

"Dear Eddie, May I just be one of the many of your admirers to congratulate you on the great record you have equalled. It is a really marvellous feat to have represented England so many times, and to have captained sides that must surely rank as some of the finest football combines ever to have represented England.

Your play has delighted me, even when I may have wished you to make a 'slip' and it is with all sincerity when I say I have picked up a few useful hints from a player who has been a credit to his club and country, and I think it is a fitting reward that the Football Association should honour you for the great services rendered.

May you have the honour of leading England many more times, so that you may go on and make a new world record. Wishing you good luck, good health and many more caps.

Yours sincerely, Andrew Beattie"

It is not often a contemporary writes in that strain, and, coming from a man who has never let his country down, it is praise indeed.

I think the only time during my whole career that I have received abusive letters was after the incident at Wembley in 1936 when I gave away a penalty against Scotland. There were only a few, but I didn't like them at all. But that minor incident doesn't in any way detract from the thousands of nice letters I have received from fans all over the world.

One contributor regularly wrote from the Gold Coast and I kept up quite a correspondence with him. But he must have thought I was made of gold because every letter contained requests for equipment, international caps, medals, etc. That finally palled. Another letter I remember was from a girl in Austria, who wrote to me c/o the hotel while we were touring. She asked would I write to her in English so that she could learn my language, while she would reply in Austrian and so teach me her native tongue. But I lost that letter on the way home, and never did learn to speak Austrian. I also had a letter from Germany, addressed Herr Hapgood, Berupsfussball-spielfuhrer, England, London! It contained a request for an autographed photo.

165

In common with other footballers I, of course, received attention from the men with an eye to what they thought was easy money. Five times I got letters offering me bribes, asking me to give away a penalty, or to fall over and let a winger cut in and score. But even had I wanted to take advantage of these 'generous' offers, I don't think they would have been worth anything, for none of the letters was signed.

The nearest I got to a concrete offer was in Switzerland, when a man wrote me, signing himself 'Well-wisher,' setting out an involved plan whereby, presumably, both he and I could make ourselves quite a nice piece of cash.

It was a detailed table to cover his bets. If I let the other side score in the first twenty minutes, I was to get so much, with additional sums for every goal scored at varying times through the game. If everything worked to plan I would net £200, and, if I agreed, I was to answer through a box number in a Swiss paper. I figured the writer was crazy or I would have handed the letter over to the authorities. But I would have liked to have had a chat with him, just to tell him that there were ten other players on the side, and, in order to carry out his plan, I would have had to let them all in on it, and, probably, also the Swiss players. So that by the time I had finished cutting up the £200, I would have been owing myself some money!

Of course, the bulk of my fan mail were requests for autographs and photographs. As many another player will agree, we usually suffer this, I nearly said menace, and, rarely is the small fan disappointed in his request. Some players, I know, however, draw the line if there is not a stamped addressed envelope sent along when a book or photo is posted to the ground or club dressing room.

One post bag brought me intense gratification, and also a lot of work. When the stories appeared of the Italian match at Highbury in which I broke my nose and played on, a headmaster of a school at Highgate got every boy of the senior class to write an essay on 'Pluck'....and then he posted the whole lot to me to correct and select the winning essay. It was a lot of hard work but I was glad to do something for the boys.

There were occasions, of course, which brought me increased post, one particularly when the press carried a couple of lines to say my wife had given birth to a son. Many of the letters I received at this time were from girls, registering disapproval that I was married, and particularly because I had a son. I thought only male film stars were supposed to remain single!

But, later, the fact of my having a son brought me a lot of correspondence of a different sort. When he was about three, a weekly picture paper carried a picture (it is included in the book) of Tony, dressed in Arsenal colours, kicking a ball at Highbury, watched by Alex James, Frank Moss and his admiring father. It is a grand picture, and so great was the demand that an extra 'edition' of the magazine had to be printed. It is, I think, my favourite picture.

That was one of the many times the Press helped me. I have always got on well with the Press. Not because I thought it policy, but because I found that if you play fair with them, they play fair with you. I have sometimes disagreed with things written about me and the games I have played in, but, on reflection, realised that their point of view, and vantage, is different entirely from mine. And maybe that they have seen things I have missed during the heat of battle.

My wife has ably carried out the self-imposed task of collecting Press cuttings and photographs: I'm glad she started. It's nice to look back, especially when memories have been pleasant, and I expect, when I'm a doddering old grandfather, I will take the cuttings and bore everybody with them.

I should like here to thank all those many friends I have made in the newspaper world, space forbids my mentioning them all by name, but particularly am I grateful to the late Jimmy Catton, L. V. Manning, Bill Kirby, the late Frank

167

Carruthers, John Macadam, Clifford Webb, and, in later years, L. N. Bailey and Roy Peskett.

To the latter especial thanks for his collaboration in this 'masterpiece.' It was born one winter's night during a six hour journey from Cardiff—surely the coldest trip I have ever made—when we walked up and down the corridor in order to keep warm, and talked football all the way.

Also my grateful thanks to Mr. S. F. Rous, Mr. George Allison and my great friend, Squadron-Leader Tom Whittaker, for the assistance they have given while I have been compiling this book, and to the various newspapers whom I wrote for permission to quote extracts.

CHAPTER 25

TESTIMONIAL

One afternoon about two years ago, I read a London evening newspaper in which the football correspondent suggested that if, and when, I beat Bob Crompton's record of 42 England soccer caps, the occasion should be recognised by the Football Association. The article went on to recall that when Bob Crompton passed the then record (held by Steve Bloomer) in 1911, he was presented with a portrait of himself in oils at a selected gathering at Blackburn the following summer.

I was interested, naturally, but paid little attention to the article, firstly because there was a war on, I was in the Services, and because I thought the Football Association would have a lot more things to think about than a presentation, and secondly, I was not sure in my mind that I had really set up a record. Remember that only thirty of my caps were gained in peacetime, and that I had been lucky enough to have been selected for twelve representative wartime England teams, which, while they were as tough as peacetime games, meant that the side was not a full representation of our national talent, owing to the service overseas of some of our players. However, I thought no more about it until Mr. S. F. Rous, secretary of the Football Association, dropped a word in my private ear that there was a likelihood of the matter being raised at a subsequent meeting of the F.A. Council.

Even then I didn't get really interested. I was too busy. While the team was awaited with some interest by the newspapermen who had started and fostered the discussion, I was in the final stages of my R.A.F. commission course at Cosford and had other things to think about besides football.

Then I got the usual letter from the F.A., saying I had been chosen to play against Wales at Wembley on January 27, 1943 (my eleventh cap against Wales, and my 43rd in all) and, for the first time, I got really excited. That selection meant I had set up a new record.

Well, the summer went by and I heard no more, until in the late autumn, I got a letter from Mr. Rous, saying that the F.A. had decided to award me a £100 testimonial as a memento of the record, and for my services to the game. This meant I was the first player ever to receive a cash presentation from the rulers of the game, and I was not only delighted, but deeply honoured that my efforts should have thus been rewarded. A far cry indeed to those days of the milk round in Bristol.

Part of the money was to be spent in assembling an album of pictures, depicting great moments in my career, and here I suspect the hand of the ever-helpful Stanley Rous, whose thoughtfulness and consideration is a byword in soccer playing circles.

Well, as I have already told you, that was my last appearance for England, a great finale. The record was made up thus (I append a full list at the end of the book): against Scotland 11 times, Wales 11, Ireland 4, Italy 3, Switzerland and Germany, two each, and one cap against the following: Hungary, Czecho-Slovakia, Holland, Austria, Belgium, Finland, France, Rest of Europe, Norway and Yugo-Slavia. In addition, I led England in two Jubilee games against Scotland and Anglo-Scots in 1935.

After serving under two captains, Goodall and Tom Cooper, I was made captain on November 14, 1934, against Italy at Highbury, and led the side for nine years on every occasion I played, except one, against Finland at Helsingfors in May 1937, when George Male was captain. Of the games I played in, England won 22, drew 6, and lost 15. Only twice did we lose by more than a goal.

What does it feel like to be awarded an England soccer cap? To me, at any rate, there was the natural excitement of being considered good enough to play for my country, the pride of achievement of a workman, the tools in this case being my feet, head and football brain, that his work was considered top-notch, and a great thankfulness that the step I had taken those years ago—to pit my youth and confidence against the masters in the game, which, while still a game, was one of those testing grounds so many fail upon—had proved myself right....I knew then that, all things being equal, I could become a great footballer, and I had, to the extent of national recognition. I was determined after receiving my first cap, that come what may, it would not be my last cap. There was the self-confidence of youth, not boasting, coming to the surface.

Notification of selection for an international team can be received in various ways, usually, of course, by letter. On most occasions we got our letters before the team was announced to the Press, a long itinerary of meeting places, and times, hotel arrangements, etc. Once or twice I have been away from home and read of my selection in the afternoon paper, but not often. The F.A. are always very thorough in their arrangements in these matters and leave nothing to chance.

In peacetime, we were well rewarded for selection in the national side. Fee was £8 per man, while we were also allowed to keep our kit, white shirt; blue shorts and blue stockings with a white ring.

Of course, you always had the option of a gold medal (value £8 8s.) in place of the fee, and that option was often exercised, especially by a first-timer. In wartime, fees were naturally reduced. Sometimes we got £4, sometimes £2, and, occasionally, savings certificates.

171

CHAPTER 26

SECOND THOUGHTS

I was once asked whether it was true that we had a compulsory saving scheme at Highbury. We had a savings scheme, but it wasn't compulsory. The idea was that we could save what we liked every week, and have our bonuses and benefits added to the scheme. When we had £1,000 to our credit, the money would be put in a trust fund by the club under our name, and Arsenal guaranteed six per cent on it. Of course, we could withdraw the money when we liked, which made it a bit too easy for some of the lads who were always coming back for a "little something to see them through the week." Still, it was a good idea, and, many of the players saved for the first time in their lives when they came to Highbury.

And so I approach the end of my tale. It has brought me a lot of fun in telling, and maybe I'll write another some day. As I have previously told, I was always glad I became a professional footballer. There were many things I disagreed with during my career. There were many times when I wanted to chuck everything and go home. I still think that a top-class player is underpaid. A man should be paid on his talent and his gate-drawing capacity, and the ceiling of £8 a week maximum should be raised. I also think a player should be given part of his transfer fee, providing a fool-proof system could be worked out whereby a player wasn't transferred every other week in order to increase his bank balance.

Once, on a train journey, in conversation with a football legislator and greybeard newspaperman, I propounded a theory whereby a player was paid on a similar scale to American sports stars....an agreed salary as a basis, and a share of the gate percentage.

172

Both had the same query.... "What about the small clubs, how would they stand up to a scheme like this?" My answer may have sounded rather brutal, "They would have to go by the board if they couldn't live in the fierce competition, or amalgamate with other clubs."

But both agreed emphatically that the scheme wouldn't work, and one finished the argument by saying that I suffered from "divine discontent", whatever that may have been.

As I have previously said, I hold strong views on training, and think that a player should train hard until he is round about the thirty mark, and then ease off slightly. By that time the benefit of the constant training will assert itself.

Hard physical training is not the only secret of success if you are to make good in the top class. Your whole life has to be regulated and purged of excess. Soccer is a hard task-master, and grants very few second chances. For the benefit of young aspirants to fame who may be on the threshold of a successful career, or the lads still at school, may I try and give you an outline of the system I have worked to during my career.

My five great "don'ts" are: wrong meals on the day of the match, ill-fitting boots, lack of protection for the shins, wrong heading of the ball, and selfishness and lack of team spirit.

The stomach plays a very important part in soccer, and lets a chap down badly if it is not in the right condition on the day of the match. In my youth, I always had a big meal an hour or so before the match....that is wrong. The general procedure is a good breakfast and a very light lunch—consisting of boiled mutton, or fish, or, what I consider best of all, a poached egg on well-crisped toast. I know that it's wartime, but those things are not prohibitive. And, anyway, you are supposed to get one egg per week most of the time!

However, to continue. If this is carried out faithfully, a great improvement will be noticed regarding your wind, and you'll find that you will be able to last out a hard match much easier. On the other hand, to try and run about with a heavy meal inside one's stomach is a thing which no sensible athlete would do. It can be dangerous. A ball hard-driven into a full stomach is not only painful, but can have serious consequences.

When watching schoolboy football, as I often do, I have noticed the very evident lack of interest taken in the condition of boots and omission of shin-guards. One must have good boots, and, by the way, studs not bars. Studs are easily the best for getting a firm grip and helping to retain balance. The boots should be well-fitting, preferably a half-size smaller than walking shoes. Professional soccer players actually wear a size smaller than their usual footwear.

The boots soon become a perfect fit, with the result that you are able to control and propel the ball with a much surer touch, and slicing and bad mis-kicks are cut down to the minimum. A goalkeeper having to take a lot of dead-ball kicks will soon notice how much more accurate his efforts will become.

Shin-guards should be worn by every young player. In the absence of these protective pads, one naturally manages to receive a painful jab or two in the course of the game. This is where the trouble begins. Bruises and cuts on the shin can often be felt for months afterwards. I can vouch for this from painful memory, after playing mixed hockey in the Air Force. I vow I will carry the scar inflicted on my shin by an enthusiastic L.A.C.W. for the rest of my life!

To improve in the art of soccer, it is imperative you should be, at least, passably skilled in 'heading' a ball. Nearly all young players appear to neglect this part of the game. Head-tennis at Highbury was inaugurated especially to help our heading.

The big fault where heading is concerned is the hunching of the shoulders, the constricted neck giving the impression of a hunchback. The result of this cramped action being painful contact on top of the head, causes the ball to bounce in any but the required direction. To correct this, the neck must be stretched out (this to obtain power), then, with the eye on the ball till the very last moment, endeavour to contact the ball square on the forehead. The ball may be travelling at great speed, but, if taken as suggested, no harm will befall the header.

And now just a word about the selfish player. Although it may be obvious that a player can carry the ball past three or four opponents, he must not cultivate this until it becomes a habit. He should be content to beat the necessary number of men and then let the ball go to a better placed colleague. Team spirit is the secret of any successful team….and so it was with Arsenal.

To my mind, you cannot combine work and play….and that applies, particularly, if you want top-class soccer. In the top-notch game you cannot hold a regular daily job or work, and still keep fit for the testing match on the Saturday.

But the dead-end system whereby a man goes out of football without a trade when his playing days are over is pernicious, and that, I contend, is one of the things the Post-War Planning Committees must tackle first. But that's for better brains than mine to wrestle with.

Meanwhile, when I come out of the Air Force, I am glad I will be able to continue in big football. A few months back I signed as manager of Blackburn Rovers. It will be totally different from playing, I know, but I am confident that Blackburn and I will get along well together. And, who knows, one day I may lead the Rovers out at Wembley for an English Cup Final with Arsenal!

To be a manager, Charlie Hewitt, late of Millwall, once said, you have to be a successful combination of football judge, psychologist, business executive, architect, accountant, lawyer, journalist, and showman. I don't know whether I am, or could be, all that, but I can always try.

Which reminds me of the time when a harassed team manager (he shall remain unknown) called in a psychologist because his lads weren't having too good a time. The psychologist, a distinguished gentleman with a million-dollar manner, called the players into a room, the door of which he locked. Then he said:

"I watched you play last Saturday, and there is nothing wrong with you. You all look 100 per cent fit, you move fast and well. The only thing wrong is that you are too anxious. You are afraid of making mistakes, with the result that you make them. Tomorrow you will go out on to the field, knowing you are a better side than your opponents. Just say to yourselves you are going to win, and it's just a matter of picking up the points."

Next day, a grand-looking, confident bunch of lads trotted out on to the field. All their opponents sensed a change in them….they looked as if they couldn't lose….they did, 0-7. There must be a moral there, but I can't find it. Anyway, it's one way of ending a book!

THE FULL RECORD

13 May 1933	v Italy, Rome	England	Drew	1-1	Goodall
20 May 1933	v Switzerland, Berne	England	Won	4-0	Goodall
14 Oct 1933	v Ireland, Belfast	England	Won	3-0	Goodall
15 Nov 1933	v Wales, Newcastle	England	Lost	1-2	Goodall
14 Apr 1934	v Scotland, Wembley	England	Won	3-0	Cooper
10 May 1934	v Hungary, Budapest	England	Lost	1-2	Cooper
16 May 1934	v Czechoslovakia, Prague	England	Lost	1-2	Cooper
29 Sept 1934	v Wales, Cardiff	England	Won	4-0	Cooper
14 Nov 1934	v Italy, Highbury	England	Won	3-2	Hapgood
6 Feb 1935	v Ireland, Liverpool	England	Won	2-1	Hapgood
6 Apr 1935	v Scotland, Glasgow	England	Lost	0-2	Hapgood
18 May 1935	v Holland, Amsterdam	England	Won	1-0	Hapgood
19 Oct 1935	v Ireland, Belfast	England	Won	3-1	Hapgood
4 Dec 1935	v Germany, Tottenham	England	Won	3-0	Hapgood
5 Feb 1936	v Wales, Wolverhampton	England	Lost	1-2	Hapgood
4 Apr 1936	v Scotland, Wembley	England	Drew	1-1	Hapgood
6 May 1936	v Austria, Vienna	England	Lost	1-2	Hapgood
9 May 1936	v Belgium, Brussels	England	Lost	2-3	Hapgood
20 May 1937	v Finland, Helsingfors	England	Won	8-0	Male
9 Apr 1938	v Scotland, Wembley	England	Lost	0-1	Hapgood
14 May 1938	v Germany, Berlin	England	Won	6-3	Hapgood
21 May 1938	v Switzerland, Zurich	England	Lost	1-2	Hapgood
26 May 1938	v France, Paris	England	Won	4-2	Hapgood
22 Oct 1938	v Wales, Cardiff	England	Lost	2-4	Hapgood
26 Oct 1938	v Rest of Europe, Highbury	England	Won	3-0	Hapgood
9 Nov 1938	v Norway, Newcastle	England	Won	4-0	Hapgood
16 Nov 1938	v Ireland, Manchester	England	Won	7-0	Hapgood
15 Apr 1939	v Scotland, Hampden	England	Won	2-1	Hapgood
13 May 1939	v Italy, Milan	England	Drew	2-2	Hapgood
18 May 1939	v Yugoslavia, Belgrade	England	Lost	1-2	Hapgood
11 Nov 1939	v Wales XI, Cardiff	England	Drew	1-1	Hapgood
13 Apr 1940	v Wales XI, Wembley	England	Lost	0-1	Hapgood
11 May 1940	v Scotland XI, Hampden	England	Drew	1-1	Hapgood
3 May 1941	v Scotland XI, Hampden	England	Won	3-1	Hapgood
7 June 1941	v Wales XI, Cardiff	England	Won	3-2	Hapgood
4 Oct 1941	v Scotland XI, Wembley	England	Won	2-0	Hapgood
25 Oct 1941	v Wales XI, Birmingham	England	Won	2-1	Hapgood
17 Jan 1942	v Scotland XI, Wembley	England	Won	3-0	Hapgood
18 Apr 1942	v Scotland XI, Glasgow	England	Lost	4-5	Hapgood
9 May1942	v Wales XI, Cardiff	England	Lost	0-1	Hapgood
10 Oct 1942	v Scotland XI, Wembley	England	Drew	0-0	Hapgood
24 Oct 1942	v Wales XI, Wolverhampton	England	Lost	1-2	Hapgood
27 Jan 1943	v Wales XI, Wembley	England	Won	5-3	Hapgood

OTHER GAMES

8 May 1935	England v Anglo-Scots, Highbury	England	Lost	0-1	Hapgood
21 Aug 1935	England v Scotland, Hampden	England	Lost	3-4	Hapgood